TRAI

British Battles Series

TRAFALGAR

OLIVER WARNER

UNABRIDGED

PAN BOOKS LTD : LONDON

First published 1959 by B. T. Batsford Ltd.
This edition published 1966 by Pan Books Ltd.,
33 Tothill Street, London, S.W.1

330 20164 6

2nd Printing 1969

*Printed in Great Britain by Richard Clay (The Chaucer Press), Ltd.,
Bungay, Suffolk*

To
W. Stanhope-Lovell
in affectionate respect

CONTENTS

ACKNOWLEDGEMENT

No account of Trafalgar could fail to be indebted to many authoritative works which have been written on the subject. The most important of these are listed chronologically, and are annotated in *Lord Nelson: a Guide to Reading* (1955) compiled by the present writer. The books which have been most often before me have been the seven volumes of Nicolas's *Dispatches and Letters of Lord Nelson* (1844–6); *Logs of the Great Sea Fights:* Vol. II (Navy Records Society 1900); Sir Henry Newbolt's *The Year of Trafalgar* (1905); Edward Fraser's *The Enemy at Trafalgar* (1906); Sir Julian Corbett's *The Campaign of Trafalgar* (1910); the Report of the Admiralty Committee on the Tactics at Trafalgar (Cd. 7120; 1913); Constance Eastwick's two-volume translation of Edouard Desbrière's *The Naval Campaign of* 1805 (1933) with its ample provision of French documentation; and the Navy Records Society edition of the *Correspondence of Lord Collingwood*, edited by Edward Hughes (1957).

In my search for fresh information I have, as so often, had the greatest help from the staff of the British Museum, the National Maritime Museum and the Admiralty Library, as well as from Rear-Admiral A. H. Taylor, whose account of the battle, published in the *Mariner's Mirror*, Vol. 36, No. 4 (October 1950), is invaluable for its concise summary of fact. I owe him much for his kindness in reading my text and allowing me the use of his notes and charts.

OLIVER WARNER

The Author and Publishers wish to thank the following for permission to include the illustrations appearing in this book:

The Board of Admiralty; Agnew and Son; The Trustees of the British Museum; Lord Cottesloe; Musée de la Marine, Paris; National Maritime Museum, Greenwich; The Parker Gallery; *Radio Times* Hulton Picture Library; The Royal United Service Institution; J. Russell and Sons; Service Historique de la Marine, Paris; Rear-Admiral A. H. Taylor, C.B. The illustration on p. xii is based on a map which appeared in *The Year of Trafalgar* by Henry Newbolt and is reproduced by permission of John Murray Ltd.

LINE DRAWINGS

ILLUSTRATIONS IN PHOTOGRAVURE

(*between pages 96 and 97*)

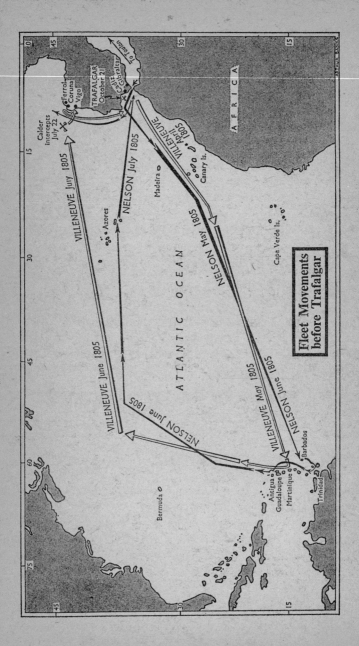

Fleet Movements before Trafalgar

1

Trafalgar: The News Breaks

FOR ITS ISSUE dated Thursday, October 24th, 1805, the *Gibraltar Chronicle* was presented with one of the biggest scoops in newspaper history – first news of Trafalgar. This came in the form of a letter from Vice-Admiral Collingwood to General Fox, Governor of the Rock, which ran as follows:

'*Euryalus*, at Sea, October 22

'Sir,

'Yesterday a Battle was fought by His Majesty's Fleet, with the Combined Fleets of Spain and France, and a Victory gained, which will stand recorded as one of the most brilliant and decisive that ever distinguished the British Navy.

'The Enemy's Fleet sailed from Cadiz, on the 19th, in the Morning, Thirty Three sail of the line in number, for the purpose of giving Battle to the British Squadron of Twenty Seven, and yesterday at Eleven A.M. the contest began, close in with the Shoals of Trafalgar.

'At Five P.M. Seventeen of the Enemy had surrendered, and one (*L'Achille*) burnt, amongst which is the *Sta. Ana*, the Spanish Admiral Don D'Alava mortally wounded, and the *Santissima Trinidad*. The French Admiral Villeneuve is now a prisoner on board the *Mars*; I believe Three Admirals are captured.

'Our loss has been great in Men; but, what is irreparable, and the cause of Universal Lamentation, is the death of the Noble Commander in Chief, who died in the Arms of Victory; I have not yet any reports from the Ships, but I have heard that Captains Duff and Cooke fell in the Action.

'I have to congratulate you upon the Great Event, and have the Honor to be, &c., &c.

C. COLLINGWOOD.'

In those days the paper was, on great occasions, printed in two parallel columns, English and French. Below Collingwood's letter were some further details, much less accurate.

'In addition to the above particulars of the late Glorious Victory, we are assured that 18 Sail of the Line were counted in our possession, before the Vessel, which brought the above dispatches, left the Fleet; and that three more of the Enemy's Vessels were seen driving about, perfect Wrecks, at the mercy of the Waves, on the Barbary Shore, and which will probably also fall into our hands.

Admiral Collingwood in the *Dreadnought* led the Van of the British Fleet most gallantly into action, without firing a shot, till his yard-arms were locked with those of the *Santissima Trinidad*; when he opened so tremendous a fire that, in fifteen minutes, she was completely dismasted, and obliged to surrender.

Lord Nelson, in the *Victory*, engaged the French Admiral most closely; during the heat of the action, his Lordship was severely wounded with a grape shot, in the side, and was obliged to be carried below. Immediately on his wound being dressed, he insisted upon being again brought upon deck, when, shortly afterwards, he received a shot through his body; he survived, however, till the Evening, long enough to be informed of the capture of the French Admiral, and of the extent of the Glorious Victory he had gained. – His last words were, *"Thank God I have outlived this day, and now I die content!"* '

There were a number of curious features about this

earliest printed report. The first was how quickly Collingwood had been faced with the onerous process of writing dispatches, once the guns had ceased to fire, in addition to managing the command to which he had succeeded. He was occupied in the same manner, without respite, for many weeks. Even the comparatively full reports which he sent to the Admiralty, and which appeared in *The Times* on November 7th, were not the end of the business, nor were the details wholly correct. A comprehensive picture emerged only gradually.

Another remarkable fact about the news was that, in spite of its immediacy, how much of it was wide of the mark; yet it had the merit of illustrating how hard it is to describe a battle until long after firing has ceased, and until those who survive, on both sides, have had the chance to compare notes. Collingwood, as was his way, was as precise as he could be, from the very first, though he was wrong about D'Alava, who not only recovered, but even preserved his flagship, which was recaptured in a sortie from Cadiz.

The supplementary details, no doubt supplied verbally by the captain of the vessel which brought the letter to the Governor, were wildly wrong. Collingwood, who did not lead the 'Van' but the 'Rear' (as he described it in his fuller account – it was really the 'Lee' line), was not in the *Dreadnought* but the *Royal Sovereign,* another three-decker. He transferred his flag to the frigate *Euryalus* because the masts of his own ship were shot away, and because the signalling in the *Euryalus,* commanded by Captain Blackwood, was the most efficient in the Fleet. He did not first engage the *Santissima Trinidad,* which probably figured in the early news simply because she happened to be the largest battle-ship then afloat. Finally Nelson, once he had received his wound, which was from a bullet, never returned to the upper deck of the *Victory,* and his last words were not quite as reported, though the printed version was in character.

Actually, when Collingwood began his dispatch, not everyone even in the victorious Fleet knew that Nelson was dead. Captain Harvey of the *Téméraire*, for instance, who had been closest in support of the Commander-in-Chief, and whose ship was very near indeed when Nelson was struck down, did not learn the news for three days, and then it came by signal from a captain in Collingwood's division.

Nevertheless, the ship that brought the tidings to Gibraltar had done well enough. She had conveyed the full momentous *effect* of the battle. There was evidence enough to give Governor Fox excuse to fire salutes, to order illuminations and to prepare to receive the victors with tempered jubilation for their achievement in adding 'a ray of Glory to His Majesty's Crown', to use a later phrase by Collingwood. It was one which he hoped would 'be attended with public benefit to our Country'.

Out in the Atlantic, beyond the Strait's Mouth, a gale was blowing, and ship after ship, scarred, dismasted and leaking, was trying to claw away from a lee shore, sometimes without success. There could be no pause for thanksgiving. Nothing but incessant work, performed with skill in the face of near-exhaustion, enabled the victors to bring in even the few prizes they were able to save – four in all. Perhaps the most remarkable result of the encounter was that not a single British ship was lost, in spite of the ravages of shot and weather. Frenchmen found this hard to believe.

It was fitting that it was to Gibraltar that the news first came of the greatest Fleet action of the Napoleonic War, and one of the last in history to be fought under sail. Gibraltar was at the door of the Mediterranean, and it was because of Villeneuve's intention to return to that sea that Nelson had been given the chance to bring him to battle. Trafalgar marked the end of the career of the most illustrious admiral in his country's history, fulfilled his wish for the annihilation of his opponents as a coherent force and secured for the Royal Navy a supremacy which was unchallenged for more than a century.

That was enough for one autumn day.

Midshipman (1799)

2

The Campaign

A FAVOURITE ANALOGY, used of the process which follows when a land-power engages in warfare against a sea-power, is to describe the matter as a tussle between an elephant and a whale. But in more recent English history what has invariably happened is that the whale has turned amphibian, while the elephant has never crossed the stretch of sea which matters most, the English Channel. The elephant has threatened; it has never been able to strike the final blow. The whale, on the other hand, while retaining mastery in its own element, has gone ashore, with aid from allied creatures, and has at last forced the elephant to come to terms.

The tussle is painful, clumsy and wasteful, like warfare in general. The classic instance occurred during the protracted war with France, which, with two short breaks, stretched from February 1793, when the Revolutionary Government declared war on Great Britain, to Waterloo, which was fought in the month of June 1815, and ended the active career of Napoleon.

The campaign which led to Trafalgar may be said to have begun when the French decided, for the second time, to mass an army on their own side of the Channel. It was, therefore, concerned with a project for invasion, since that idea was at one time dominant in Napoleon's mind. But neither the campaign nor its culminating engagement saved England from the threat, because its realization was in fact never likely. Channel supremacy, at least temporarily, was essential to success, and that supremacy remained British. Before Trafalgar was fought Napoleon, despairing of his seamen, had faced his army about, and had engaged in operations which led to French triumphs at Ulm and Austerlitz, deep in the heart of Continental Europe.

Yet in order to understand both campaign and battle, it is necessary to follow the threads of Napoleon's scheme, to trace the counter-measures, and to perceive how the retention of sea supremacy turned what appeared to be a defensive campaign into one which broke the Franco-Spanish Navy, forced Napoleon into maritime guerilla warfare which could irritate but which could not be decisive and enabled Great Britain to retain that foothold in the Mediterranean which was one of the principles of her strategy.

Trafalgar did not save England: she was always inviolate while her Fleet remained undefeated. It reinforced her naval 'combat supremacy' – to use a well-known phrase of Admiral Mahan's – and it ensured that she retained a springboard in the Mediterranean, in far-away Sicily, from which Napoleon himself could be threatened. It was an offensive, not a defensive success.

A plan for invasion had been in Napoleon's mind at least since the year 1798, when he had paid a brief visit to Dunkirk and the Flemish coast. He had then concluded that the idea was too hazardous to be attempted, except as a last desperate measure.

'Whatever efforts we make,' he reported to the French Government, 'we shall not for some years gain the naval supremacy. To invade England without that supremacy is the most daring and difficult task ever undertaken. . . . If, having regard to the present organisation of our navy, it seems impossible to gain the necessary promptness of execution, then we must really give up the expedition, be satisfied with keeping up the pretence of it, and concentrate all our attention and resources on the Rhine, in order to try to deprive England of Hanover and Hamburg . . . or else undertake an eastern expedition which would menace her trade with the Indies. And if none of these three operations is practicable, I see nothing else for it but to conclude peace. . . .'

Napoleon's career was an illustration of the truth of his report. The plan for invasion, which he then judged impracticable, was a threat which would always engage a high proportion of England's resources; the matter of British interests in Germany was one which, in due time, a successful French policy could determine; while he himself was soon to lead an 'eastern expedition' which gained him Egypt, and might have taken him to the gates of India had not Nelson destroyed his Fleet at the battle of the Nile, isolated his troops and left them to become the victim of one of the earlier amphibious triumphs of the war.

Despite his low view of the prospects of success, Napoleon revived the scheme of invasion in the spring and summer of 1801, and assembled flotillas and an army at Boulogne to train for the attempt. Nelson, fresh from a campaign in the Baltic, was given command of a force of small vessels, stationed at strategic points from Orfordness to Beachy Head, which were to destroy the enterprise should it ever leave France.

Never defensively minded, Nelson was always for what he called the 'home stroke', and on August 15th, 1801, he made a bold attempt at capturing the French craft as they lay in harbour.

'When any boats have taken one vessel,' so ran his orders, 'the business is not to be considered as finished, but a sufficient number being left to guard the prize, the others are immediately to pursue the object by proceeding to the next, and so on until the whole Flotilla be either taken or wholly annihilated, for there must not be the smallest cessation until their destruction is completely finished. . . .'

The orders typify Nelson's whole attitude to war. The

old days of stately, formal challenge were, in his eyes, gone for good. The only way to fight Napoleon was to be as ruthless as he was, and equally skilful. Annihilation was his purpose.

In fact, the assault was repulsed with loss, to the mortification of Nelson and the jubilation of the enemy – but the gallantry with which it was carried out gave the French a shrewd notion of what they might expect if they ever put to sea in force.

The army remained massed at Boulogne until the signing of the Treaty of Amiens in 1802, which marked the first of the two short breaks in the war. When the conflict was resumed, after exactly a year, Napoleon detained every male Briton aged between eighteen and sixty who happened to be in France, an act which caused a general outcry throughout the civilized world, since hitherto any noncombatant overtaken by hostilities in enemy territory had been safe from molestation. He also concentrated much of his powerful energy on a renewal of the threat upon the island which he could see so plainly from his northern clifftops.

He pushed forward preparations in all available dockyards of France, Holland and Northern Italy. The great mole which had been planned to shelter the roadstead at Cherbourg was continued, and the entire littoral, from the Seine to the Rhine, became 'a coast of iron and bronze'. Troops were withdrawn from distant frontiers and encamped along the shores of Picardy; others were stationed in reserve at St Omer, Montreuil, Utrecht and elsewhere, while concentrations were made at Ghent, Compiègne and St Malo. Bodies of men at Boulogne, Etaples, Wimereux and Ambleteuse formed the spear-head of the Grand Army with which Napoleon proposed to conquer the stubborn islanders. England might well have trembled, since she could see gigantic preparation and was battered with incessant propaganda: actually, she did nothing of the sort

She rearmed, she prepared, she waited. The idea of invasion was an old one: Philip of Spain had tried it with his Armada in 1588; the Dutch had boldly sailed up the Medway in the following century; it had been a recurring project with the French.

> 'But the most remarkable feature of the time,' wrote Sir Henry Bunbury, who was then serving as an army officer, 'was the flame which burst forth and spread its light over the whole of Britain. It was not merely the flame of patriotism, or of indignation at the bare idea that England should lie at the proud foot of a conqueror; it appeared to be fed and rendered intense by a passionate hatred of Napoleon personally.'

It was hatred that the writer emphasized, not alarm. *'Never fear the event!'* That had been Nelson's summing up in 1801. If pressed, he would probably have agreed with the famous remark of old Lord St Vincent. 'I don't say the enemy cannot come; I only say they cannot come by sea!'

Although such optimism was justified, yet while the French fleet remained undefeated in battle, the threat of a descent by the Grand Army hung like a distant cloud. To meet the enemy at sea was a major object in the Trafalgar campaign.

II

Admiralty dispositions to counter Napoleon's land concentration were traditional; experience had proved them effective. Facing the army of invasion from the Texel to Havre was a swarm of sloops and gun-vessels, rendering the passage of flotillas impossible without the support of ships of the line. A small battle-squadron under Lord Keith, with his headquarters in the Downs, and with secondary bases at Great Yarmouth and the Nore, provided a covering force. There was an independent cruiser squadron under Saumarez, based on the Channel Islands, which not only prevented the passage of hostile transports from that quarter but acted as a link between Keith and the main British fleet. This fleet was Cornwallis's western squadron, whose purpose was to contain the enemy at Brest, to secure the entrance to the Channel and to provide a focal point for outlying squadrons watching ports such as Rochefort.

Cornwallis's force was the core of Britain's defence. It exercised a close blockade of Brest: its other duty was trade protection, and guardianship of the whole Channel position. Until the enemy defeated Cornwallis, invasion was impossible. If any of his outlying ships were forced to retreat by the appearance of an independent or an escaping squadron superior in numbers it was the duty of the commanding officer to join the nearest British detachment, and to await reinforcement, remembering always that the key position was the western approach to the Channel. 'We are aware that many circumstances may occur to which these instructions are inapplicable, and for which no provision is made.' So ran the orders to Cornwallis. 'In these cases you must use your discretion and judgement for your guidance, giving us the earliest information of your proceedings. . . .' The principles of maritime strategy in home waters were so well understood that latitude could be allowed; they held good for the entire campaign.

On renewal of war Nelson had been given the command in the Mediterranean, and kept continual though generally distant watch on Toulon throughout the later part of the year 1803 and the whole of the following year, often with meagre forces, never setting foot ashore, and without the excitement of a general action. Before the close of 1804 Napoleon had secured an ally in Spain, which country brought him a nominal increase of thirty-two ships of the line. With the Dutch Fleet also arrayed against Britain, the Navy's margin of strength was then barely superior.

It was in fact questionable how much additional strength
the Spanish would afford the enemy at sea. Their ships
were well built but ill-manned, and their war record, in the
earlier stages of the struggle, had been indifferent. Nevertheless, one of the first steps taken by Pitt's Government
after the advent of the new combination had been to form a
'Spanish Squadron' under Sir John Orde, whose sphere
was to be between the Straits of Gibraltar and Cape Finisterre, with the particular duty of watching Cadiz. For
various reasons, this was annoying to Nelson. Orde was
senior to him, and he was in the best possible position to
gather prize-money; moreover, the new disposition divided
Nelson's command, which by tradition extended as far as
Cape St Vincent. The appointment itself was reasonable
enough, in view of Nelson's application for leav_ to come
home on account of his health, an application which had
actually been granted. But the entrance of Spain into the
war determined him not to leave his station. New dangers
and difficulties revived his spirits. The bigger the problem,
the more his mind rejoiced in finding a solution. It was not
long before he was faced with the first of many, for in
January 1805 Villeneuve escaped from Toulon.

On January 17th, 1805, the French put to sea with
eleven of the line and nine frigates. No one knew their
intended destination, which was in fact the West Indies,
Admiral Missiessy having also escaped from Rochefort
under orders to make his way thither. Napoleon's scheme at
this time may have been an expedition against British
possessions in the Caribbean, not a concentration to be
formed with the object of returning to Europe and ensuring
a chance of invasion. For the moment invasion plans were
dormant.

Two British frigates shadowed the enemy until they
were in the latitude of Ajaccio. There they made for the
Maddelena anchorage at the northerly tip of Sardinia,
which was Nelson's rendezvous. They reported that they

had left the enemy standing south-south-west.

Nelson, in common with most of Europe, considered that Napoleon's immediate object was the subjugation of all Italy, and he knew that the security of sea communications in the Mediterranean hung largely upon the integrity of Sicily. In the dead of night, and in a north-westerly gale, he led his fleet through the perilous Biche Passage and down the eastern coast of Sardinia, in order to bar Villeneuve's way east.

Having reached the southern end of Sardinia, Nelson was faced with a heavy westerly gale which held him there until the 26th, when his frigates began to come in from renewed searches. They brought no news except that at least one of Villeneuve's ships had been disabled by heavy weather. Nelson now felt sure that the French had either put back to Toulon or, favoured by the weather, had swept round him to attack Greece or Egypt. These countries were second only to Naples, Sardinia and Sicily in the defensive function that had been assigned to him, and he therefore held away eastwards. In Greece all seemed quiet, but there was information that the French ambassador had just been recalled from Constantinople, which might indicate that Villeneuve's destination was Egypt. Nelson therefore carried on to Alexandria. Once again there were no signs of the enemy.

Villeneuve, meanwhile, had found that his ships, manned with inexperienced seamen and encumbered with troops, were unable to face the heavy weather. All was havoc aloft, the fleet began to scatter, and the French admiral, oppressed with the consciousness that wherever his enemy might be he would be spoiling for a fight, felt it madness to proceed. He consulted General Lauriston, who was in command of the troops, and together they decided to turn back. 'Finding ourselves observed from the first night of our getting out by the two English frigates,' Villeneuve wrote to the Emperor, 'which could not fail to

Admiral Villeneuve. From a contemporary engraving

bring down upon us the whole force of the enemy, and it being out of our power to make much sail with the ships so much maltreated, we agreed to return.'

By January 21st the French were once more snug in Toulon, while Nelson, cleared for action, was waiting for them at the south of Sardinia. Although Villeneuve had succeeded in getting away, he had failed to profit by it, and Napoleon immediately informed Missiessy that his operations, henceforward, were independent. Nelson's vain search had depressed his spirits, though he found some consolation in the efficiency of his ships. When the alarm was over he wrote to his friend Collingwood: 'Bonaparte has often made his brags that our Fleet would be worn out by keeping the sea – that his was kept in order and increasing by staying in port; but now he finds, if Emperors hear truth, that his Fleet suffers more in one night, than ours in one year.'

No informed person blamed Nelson for the fact that Villeneuve had got away – he always insisted that this was his wish, since it gave him the chance to defeat him in the open sea, preferably at some distance from his base. 'I beg to inform your Lordship,' he once wrote to the Lord Mayor of London, 'that the port of Toulon has never been blockaded by me, quite the reverse – every opportunity has been offered to the enemy to put to sea, for it is there that we hope to realize the hopes and expectations of our country. . . .' What had foiled him was the fact that both his look-outs had been driven off at the same time, due to the number and activity of the enemy's light forces. But he still held command of the Mediterranean.

III

Thwarted in one plan by the failure of Villeneuve, Napoleon quickly embarked on another, which has become known as his grand design for the campaign. He had been encouraged by the energy which Spain had shown in her preparations for war, and to the Spanish Government he gave an early indication of his scheme.

On February 27th, 1805, Missiessy, in the West Indies, was ordered to stay where he was, at least until the end of June, and to be in immediate readiness to join other forces which would in due course appear off Martinique. On the same day Admiral Gourdon, who commanded a French force at Ferrol, was told to be ready to come out with such Spanish ships as were prepared for sea, and to combine with a squadron which would appear before the port. This squadron was to be Ganteaume's, the admiral who held the command at Brest.

Ganteaume was ordered to embark some three thousand troops over and above those already serving as marines, and to sail at the earliest possible moment with twenty-one of the line, six frigates and two store-ships carrying provisions for Gourdon.

He was to make straight for Ferrol, driving away the blockading squadron under Sir Robert Calder. He was then to summon Gourdon by signal, and proceed with him to Martinique, where he would find Missiessy and Villeneuve awaiting him. Ganteaume was to reinforce the Martinique garrison with a thousand troops, and, with the forty sail of the line which he would by then have collected under his command, he was to return at once to Europe. Off Ushant he was to overwhelm any British force he might find there, and push on to Boulogne, where he would be expected by about the middle of July. In the event of Villeneuve failing to leave the Mediterranean, Ganteaume was to wait thirty days, and then, though he would have only twenty-five sail of the line instead of forty, he was still to try to fight his way through to Boulogne. If for any reason he found himself with less than this number, then he was to rendezvous off Ferrol, where there would be a concentration of all the

French and Spanish naval forces in Europe. He was then to make for the Channel.

Villeneuve's orders, when he had broken out of the Mediterranean, were to relieve the blockade of Cadiz, to release the Spanish ships in that port and proceed with them to Martinique. Once there, he was to hold his squadron for forty days in readiness to come out on a signal from Ganteaume. At the end of that time, if Ganteaume had not appeared, he was to land his troops in the French islands, do what harm he could to British interests and take station off the Canaries, on the route to the East Indies. Possibly Ganteaume might meet him there, but if Ganteaume did not appear within twenty days, then Villeneuve was to return to Cadiz, where he would be given further orders. In Villeneuve's case no provision was made for the concentration at Ferrol, but possibly it was Napoleon's intention to arrange for this when the situation had developed further.

The idea was simple and admirable on paper, but it was that of a soldier. What his admirals thought of it is not on record, which is perhaps as well. When, during the present century, the scheme came to be scrutinized by the French general staff they concluded: 'Such a plan would be unworthy both of Napoleon and his genius, if we could discover nothing deeper in it.' What can be discovered 'deeper' is a way whereby a dictator could save his face. If his combinations failed, the blame would not be upon his own head, but on that of his navy. 'Englishmen with judgement unoppressed by the Napoleonic legend,' says Sir Julian Corbett, 'will see in it the work of a self-confident amateur in naval warfare, the blindness of a great soldier to the essential differences between land and sea strategy, and something perhaps of the exasperated despot who refused to own himself beaten.' Napoleon blithely ignored the winds, and the obvious counter-moves by the enemy. In fact, he dismissed the possibility of serious opposition until a combination of his squadrons presented themselves in overwhelming superiority. He could admire the neatness of his own scheme, unbothered by any problems of practical application. These were a matter for the sailors; his part was to give them orders.

'It is grievous to me to know the naval profession,' wrote Decrès, the French Minister of Marine, to his imperial master, 'since this knowledge wins no confidence, nor produces any result in Your Majesty's combinations.' Poor Decrès put the matter neatly. Napoleon's assumptions were outrageous, but no one was in a position to tell him so, and if they had been it would have made no difference. It almost appeared as if he was bent on sacrificing his Navy, and incidentally that of Spain, for the slender chance of bringing about an invasion in which he had himself begun to lose hope.

In point of fact Napoleon had reason to hold the British Navy in less regard than did his admirals. He had made a name for himself as a young artillery officer by helping to drive Hood's ships and men from Toulon, which was opened to them by royalists early in the Revolutionary war, and held for a time as an enclave in hostile territory. He had sailed the Mediterranean at the centre of a strong fleet, taking Malta on the way to his successful landing in Egypt. Although his flagship and all but two of his battle squadron had been sunk by Nelson, he himself, months later, had successfully evaded the British blockade, sailing back to France in a frigate commanded by Ganteaume. As for Villeneuve, he credited him with being lucky: not only had he escaped from the holocaust of the Nile with his 80-gun ship, *Le Guillaume Tell*, but he had shown that it was possible to elude Nelson's watch. If his luck held, he might do this again.

The Admiralty in London at first suspected nothing of the scope of the grand design, but from every blockade port there came signs of activity. Off Ferrol, Calder had news that the enemy squadron was ordered to be ready to sail by

was the Gulf of Palmas, at the southerly tip of Sardinia. Villeneuve then had one of the greatest pieces of luck in his entire cruise. He spoke to a neutral merchantman, who told him exactly where Nelson was. During the night Villeneuve altered course to pass inside the Balearics. This movement caused the frigates to lose touch, and the French were able to run clear down the coast of Spain, and right out of Nelson's ken. Nelson's counter-action was to spread his forces to bar Villeneuve's way east, and to wait for certain news. His principal duty, then as always, was guardianship of the Mediterranean.

Although only a part of Napoleon's plan, and that the most doubtful, seemed to have succeeded, the campaign of Trafalgar was well and truly under way. On April 7th, while Nelson was waiting near Ustica, Villeneuve was becalmed off Barcelona. There he could see a Spanish squadron of six of the line under Salcedo, who would have been willing enough to have had his company to Cadiz if the French could have waited for Salcedo to receive positive orders to move, and given him time to get his powder on board. But in the evening an easterly breeze sprang up, ideal for a run to the Straits of Gibraltar, and Villeneuve, uncertain where Nelson was, dared not wait. He left the Cartagena squadron isolated, and made for the Atlantic, which he entered on April 9th (see map, p. 12).

At Cadiz Admiral Gravina, with fifteen of the line, was waiting for the French, but only a proportion of his ships were ready for sea, and he was watched by Orde, though with an inferior force. The first news that Orde had of Villeneuve's escape was from Sir Richard Strachan in the *Renown*. He came under press of sail to say that he had actually seen the French off Gibraltar. Had it not been for this warning, Orde, who was provisioning, believed that he would have been surprised and destroyed.

Orde had by then heard of Ganteaume's activity at Brest and shrewdly guessed that what was in Napoleon's mind was a massing of his squadrons at some distant rendezvous. He himself had not the force to remain off Cadiz, and as he moved away he sent an urgent appreciation to the Admiralty. 'I am persuaded,' he said, 'the enemy will not remain long at Cadiz, and I think the chances are great in favour of their destination being westward, where, by a sudden concentration of several detachments, Bonaparte may hope to gain a temporary superiority in the Channel, and, availing himself of it, to strike his enemy a mortal blow.' Orde intended to follow traditional strategy by falling back towards the Western squadron. 'In bringing to England the larger ships under my command,' he said, 'I shall afford an opportunity to dispose of them anew; by which little can be risked, and much might be gained if the enemy's blow is aimed at England or Ireland.' He ordered his cruisers to warn blockaders in the northerly positions, sent off a ship to the West Indies with information that the French were at large in the Atlantic and arranged for the *Amphion,* a fast sailer, to keep in touch with the enemy.

Late on April 9th the French were off Cadiz, and Villeneuve signalled Gravina to come out. In his eagerness to hide his tracks Villeneuve dared not sacrifice the darkness of a single night, and after waiting less than four hours he held away, leaving his allies to straggle out as best they could. The movement was so speedy that the *Amphion* had no chance to begin her watch.

Villeneuve and Gravina were gone, and from the moment they left Cadiz were lost to British eyes. They had the world before them, and only off Ushant was there a force capable of bringing them to battle successfully. When messengers from Spain sped to Napoleon with the news of the first powerful joining of squadrons the Emperor had every reason to be pleased. He had been right in his faith in Villeneuve. He had misled the most dreaded of his opponents, and had evaded the others. It must have seemed to

Napoleon that at no time, since he had first contemplated the idea of invasion, had it had a better prospect of success.

I V

Only one thing could have been calculated to please Napoleon as much as Villeneuve's escape, and that was the existing state of affairs in London. There, in spite of an impassioned defence by Pitt, his friend Lord Melville had been forced from office after the revelation that serious irregularities had been permitted in the handling of Admiralty funds, for which, as First Lord, Melville was responsible. For a time the Admiralty was without a head, and that at a crisis in the war.

Pitt would have been in desperation had there not been an officer capable of taking the helm, though it was improbable that the appointment could be of long duration. Sir Charles Middleton, the man in question, had made a high reputation as Controller of the Navy. Although nearly eighty, he was prepared in the emergency to serve as First Lord, and was most fitted to do so. He was raised to the peerage as Lord Barham, and at once took over strategical control of the Fleet. It was not a moment too soon. Craig was at sea, Villeneuve was out and no squadron had yet received orders to cover the passage of the transports. Knight, with his two ships of the line, could have put up no serious defence if the French appeared in strength, and the capture or destruction of Craig's army would have been felt as a national disgrace.

The first news Barham received that the Combined French and Spanish squadron was at large came through the alertness of Lord Mark Kerr, a frigate captain who had been refitting at Gibraltar when Villeneuve passed through the Straits. It came on April 25th, just a week after Craig had sailed. On the same day there issued a series of prescient orders from Barham.

First to be warned was Sir Alexander Cochrane in the West Indies. If he could concentrate all the detachments already in that area at Fort Royal, Jamaica, there would be eleven of the line, including one three-decker, which was a force strong enough to hold the Combined Fleet in check until reinforcements could arrive. Preliminary orders were followed by others, which are best described as contingent. A military force was in process of passing through seas where no decision had as yet taken place. The chain of covering squadrons had been disrupted, therefore the expedition itself must be withdrawn, unless it had already passed the danger point. If, however, the enemy movement was found not to endanger it, it must be assumed that the threat was aimed at the point of greatest stress. That point was the western end of the Channel, the permanent focal point of strategy.

During all this time nothing had been heard from Nelson, and Sir Richard Strachan's conjecture that he had once more gone to Egypt was accepted, for want of other news. In fact, in his perplexity, Nelson had resolved not to go to the eastward of Sicily or the westward of Sardinia until he knew something positive of the enemy. Then he heard, for the first time, about Craig and his army. His official notification of its movements had been delayed, and, although at first Nelson had nothing to go upon but rumour, this was soon followed by a letter from Elliot, the British Minister at Naples, which confirmed the news. But if it was true that Craig was at sea, then the true danger zone was the mouth of the Straits of Gibraltar. To increase his dilemma, persistent heavy weather from the west delayed progress in that direction. Finally, through one of his own cruisers, he had certain news that Villeneuve had passed through the Straits on April 8th. His cup of disappointment was full; but at least he was no longer uncertain what his own course should be. He disposed a light squadron for the protection of the Mediterranean, and pushed his way westward at the best pace his ships could manage.

Even when he reached Gibraltar, Nelson did not, at first, find it easy to make up his mind where to take his ships. His first instinct was to head north, to reinforce the Channel Fleet. Then he heard that Knight and Craig had put into the Tagus, somewhat to the embarrassment of the Portuguese, who were maintaining a precarious neutrality. News had come – false, as it happened – that Villeneuve had put back into Cadiz, and if that was so, it would have been madness for Craig to proceed.

No one landed in Portugal, not even the commander-in-chief on the usual visit of courtesy, while as a precaution a plan was made for troops to surprise and seize a fort commanding the main channel, if the French should appear at the approaches to Lisbon.

By May 10th the rumour of the return to Cadiz was shown to be groundless, and the expedition again put to sea. Off Cape St Vincent contact was made with Nelson. By that time the admiral had had private information from an English officer in Portuguese service of the probable destination of the Combined Squadron. Nelson directed Knight to take the transports wide of Cadiz and Tarifa, and then to run straight along the Moorish coast into Gibraltar. Despite his relative inferiority to his prospective enemy, he handed over the three-decked *Royal Sovereign* to reinforce Craig's escort. He knew it to be essential that the Army should have the fullest possible protection, while on passage in the Mediterranean, against a sortie from Cartagena. 'He seems to have acted most handsomely,' wrote Lord Hardwicke, 'as indeed he always does for the public service, in weakening his own force for the security of the country.'

Nelson then bore up on his long chase westward, with ten of the line and three frigates. On May 14th, as he approached Madeira, he wrote to the Admiralty giving them his intentions, adding that even if Villeneuve was not where he supposed him to be, little harm could come from his own course of action. As he said, if his opponent was not in fact in the West Indies, 'the squadron will be back again by the end of June – in short, before the enemy can know where I am.'

V

Meanwhile all had not gone smoothly with French plans. Missiessy, who had begun his West Indian foray in hope, had met with no sister squadrons to his own, and by May 20th he had returned to Rochefort, sick and dispirited. He had done som.. damage to British interests in the Caribbean, and Cochrane had missed encountering him, but, though he had tried, he had not removed the thorn and shame of the Governor of Martinique. This was a rugged cone, barely a mile from the south-west point of the principal French island, which had been captured in 1803 by Samuel Hood, and been fancifully placed in the Navy List as HM sloop *Diamond Rock*. The cone had been manned for two years by a party of seamen under Commander James Maurice, who had led an adventure-story existence, raiding, cutting-out and proving themselves a running sore to garrison and shipping. Missiessy's failure, during the weeks of his cruise, to dispose of Maurice exasperated Frenchmen from Napoleon downwards. 'I choked with indignation,' wrote the Emperor to his Minister of Marine, 'when I read he had not taken the Diamond.'

It was left for Villeneuve to remove the menace. The Combined Squadron appeared off Martinique on May 14th – with a month's start of Nelson. Maurice's greeting was to entice one of the Spanish ships of the line close to the rock by hoisting French colours, a legitimate ruse of war, and to salute her with shot. Villeneuve then set about him in earnest, with two ships of the line, three frigates, gunboats and

a force of troops. Maurice held out until June 6th, by
which time he had not a cartridge or a drop of water left.
His defence had given time for pursuers to close up; it had
also enabled a fast ship to arrive with orders from Paris.
Her captain reported that Ganteaume, though hourly expected to leave Brest, had not yet done so, that Nelson had
'gone to Egypt' and that, although Missiessy had vanished,
two of the line and eight hundred soldiers had left Rochefort under Magon and should be near at hand. Villeneuve
was ordered to stay for thirty days after Magon's arrival,
then, if Ganteaume had not come, he was to return to
Ferrol. Meanwhile he was not to waste time, but to operate
against the British colonies.

The day after Diamond Rock fell Magon appeared, but
Nelson, with his ten of the line, was by then off Barbados.
Returning to the West Indies after eighteen years it seemed
at first that he had the chance of a battle on the scale of
Rodney's famous action in 1782. But luck was still with
Villeneuve. Nelson, it is true, was joined by Cochrane with
two of the line, which brought his numbers up to twelve,
but he also had news from General Brereton, commanding
at St Lucia, that Villeneuve had been seen on a course
which would take him to Trinidad. Nelson, though his own
instinct was to disbelieve the intelligence, dared not dis-
regard evidence from an officer whom he had known of old,
and trusted. He headed his ships south. The news seemed
to be confirmed next day by word from the *Curieux* brig,
which was scouting ahead.

As he came within sight of Trinidad Nelson was himself
mistaken for the enemy; outposts fired their block-houses
behind them, and Nelson pushed through into the Gulf of
Paria believing that he had before him a second battle of
the Nile, with the French and Spaniards caught embayed.
He found nothing.

The tragi-comedy of mistaken identity was soon cleared
up, and Nelson, casting all 'intelligence' to the winds, acted

on his own judgement, and once more hurried back north. He had scarcely left Trinidad when he had news from Maurice that the Combined Squadron were still at Martinique. Maurice had been told by his captors that the Ferrol squadron had recently joined them; but about this Nelson felt doubts, since Maurice himself would surely have seen them. 'Powerful as their force may be,' he wrote to the Governor of Barbados, 'mine is compact, theirs must be unwieldy, and although a very pretty fiddle I don't believe that either Gravina or Villeneuve know how to play upon it.'

The next authentic item of news was that Villeneuve had also headed north – he had been seen off Guadeloupe. 'Whether the enemy's object is to attack Antigua or St Kitts,' said Nelson, 'or to return to Europe, time will show.' He himself carried on, under press of sail, in the same general direction. He was not able to prevent the one further success of Villeneuve's cruise, the capture of fourteen merchantmen, homeward bound, under the escort of a single schooner, but the gap between the squadrons was closing.

At Antigua Nelson, knowing that his active presence had ensured the safety of the British islands and the bulk of the shipping, formed the opinion that the enemy were returning to Europe. The matter was clinched by the arrival of the schooner which had accompanied the luckless convoy. Having escaped his pursuers, her captain was able to report the course and strength of the Combined Squadron, and Nelson knew that he was now only three or four days behind his opponent. At once he made ready to re-cross the Atlantic, ordering the *Curieux* to proceed ahead at her best speed, with the latest news for the Admiralty. On her way Bettesworth, her captain, sighted Villeneuve on a northerly course, evidently making for the Bay of Biscay rather than the Straits of Gibraltar.

Bettesworth anchored his brig at Plymouth on July 7th,

reported to the local admiral and at once posted to London. He reached the Admiralty at eleven o'clock on the night of the 8th, to find that Barham had retired. No one dared disturb him. In the morning, when he heard who had arrived, the First Lord was furious that even an hour had been wasted. Without waiting to dress, he issued instructions to dispose the fleet to meet the return of the enemy. It was likely that a clash might take place off Cape Finisterre, so Sir Robert Calder, who was then off Ferrol, must be reinforced. The squadron off Rochefort was ordered to his support, and Cornwallis, who was back from sick-leave, was told to 'stretch with the Fleet under your immediate command' in a south-westerly direction, an order which he had already anticipated.

These moves, to divide the Fleet, were stigmatized by Napoleon as *insigne bêtise* – stupidity of a remarkable kind. They certainly opened Brest, which was watched only by a cruiser squadron, and they allowed a vigorous new commander, Allemand, the chance to escape from Rochefort; one which he duly took. Now, if ever, was the time for Ganteaume to act swiftly. He should make at once for Boulogne – so said Napoleon. 'There all is prepared, and there, master of the sea for three days, you will enable us to end the destiny of England. . . . When you receive this letter we shall be in person at Boulogne, and all will be on board and moored alongside.'

But before Ganteaume could make ready Cornwallis, having run his 'stretch' without sight of Villeneuve, was back in position. The Brest fleet was held fast within its port, and it was Calder who, on July 22nd, met the Combined Squadron in what could have been a dress rehearsal for Trafalgar, or what could even have made that battle unnecessary.

Calder's action, fought in a mist and therefore in increasing confusion, was inconclusive. The admiral himself described it as 'very decisive', while, for his part, Villeneuve reported 'cries of joy and victory are heard from all our ships!' In fact Calder, facing a fleet superior in numbers, captured two Spaniards, inflicted otherwise more damage than he sustained and prevented Villeneuve, at least for the time, from gaining Ferrol. But it was not enough. He had achieved little more than a creditable brush in the old style of encounter.

It was a poor result for being directed to the right place at the right time. For his failure to make every possible effort to renew action next day, and 'to take and destroy every ship of the enemy', Calder was reprimanded. But by the time judgement was delivered Trafalgar had been fought and won, and a new standard established, so that Calder may be said to have fought within one tradition and to have been censured within a greater. He himself was pained at the disappointment felt in England after the action. In fact it had wrecked Barham's careful plans. The enemy fleet was still together: two prizes weighed not a straw in his consideration, and the crisis of the campaign had not yet been resolved. Villeneuve, who had made for Vigo, might still move north or south, towards the Channel or the Mediterranean, and Barham's irritation at Calder's idea that his services should be publicly recognized was, in the circumstances, natural enough.

'It is, as Mr Pitt knows, annihilation that the country wants, and not merely a splendid victory . . . honourable to the parties concerned, but absolutely useless in the extended scale to bring Bonaparte to his marrow bones. . . .' The words were Nelson's, but he belonged to a school of thought to which bravery by itself was not enough. Bravery was taken for granted in such men as Calder. Napoleon's conception was Total War: it was one with which Nelson had long been familiar, and one for which he had prepared ever since the conflict opened.

VI

Making for Cape St Vincent in case Villeneuve's destination should be Cadiz, Nelson reached the coast of Spain, as he had hoped, before the enemy. On July 20th he set foot ashore, at Gibraltar, for the first time in almost two years. Though he remained baulked of his quarry, he had at least some news to cheer him. The Mediterranean was safe, and he found Collingwood off Cadiz, in command of a watching squadron.

In Nelson's absence Collingwood and Bickerton between them had ensured Craig a safe passage to Malta; the transports had in fact anchored at Valetta three days before Nelson reached the Straits, though it was weeks before he knew it. It was Collingwood's view that Villeneuve's object was to bring out the Ferrol squadron and make for Ushant. Nelson was unsure. He re-disposed what ships there were in the Mediterranean to give greater safety to Malta, and had scarcely sent off his orders when a sloop, fresh from England, brought news of what the *Curieux* had reported. Nelson could no longer be in doubt. If Villeneuve had been making for the Bay, then to the Bay he would go. Winds forced him to a westerly course, and he met nothing. Leaving the greater part of his squadron to reinforce Cornwallis, he himself, with the worn-out *Superb* in company, made for Spithead, where he anchored on August 18th, very doubtful of the reception he would meet with from his countrymen. He had guessed wrong more than once, and he could scarcely have been surprised (though he affected to be pained) that Barham sent for the *Victory*'s journal. When the old seaman read the day-to-day particulars of Nelson's chase, any questions as to the soundness of his conduct were fully answered – though Nelson's luck was another matter. His professional reputation remained where it had stood since the Nile. As for his countrymen, their joy at his return, their respect for his zeal and devotion over the weary and frustrated months at sea, made it almost seem as if he had won a victory.

The atmosphere was prophetic, for at five o'clock on the morning of September 2nd, when Nelson was at his country house at Merton, conveniently close to the road from Portsmouth to the Admiralty, a post-chaise drove up to the door bringing Captain Henry Blackwood of the frigate *Euryalus*. Nelson was already dressed, and on seeing Blackwood, who had served him with distinction on earlier occasions, he exclaimed, 'I am sure you bring me news of the French and Spanish Fleets, and I think I shall yet have to beat them!'

It was true enough. What Blackwood had to tell him was that Villeneuve had struggled from Vigo to Ferrol, where, with the Spaniards, he mustered a combined force of thirty of the line. He had later, it seemed, attempted to obey his master's orders by heading for Brest, but had met with a strong north-easter, and had turned his ships for Cadiz. His action killed the last remaining hope of invasion. Napoleon, realizing at last the futility of his grand design, made preparations to break up his camp, and to employ his army in a land campaign.

Villeneuve, who had left Ferrol on August 13th, was off Cadiz a week later, his force increased by the Spanish ships already blockaded in that port. Collingwood, who at the time was in no strength to prevent it, having but three of the line with him, allowed the enemy undisputed entry, but at once returned to a watching position. 'They are in the port like a forest,' he wrote calmly to his sister. 'I reckon them now to be thirty-six sail of the line and plenty of frigates. What can I do with such a host? But I hope I shall get a reinforcement, suited to the occasion and, if I do, well betide us!' He knew that, once fresh ships reached him, Villeneuve could not drive through the Straits without challenge, and, given fair conditions, not at all.

Collingwood did not have long to wait, for Cornwallis

made a new disposition which would certainly have ranked, in Napoleon's eyes, as a further *insigne bêtise*, and a detachment under Calder arrived before Cadiz only eleven days after the Combined Fleet.

Of the French squadrons, only Allemand's was now at large, but his force, though sufficient for a raid, and brilliantly used in commerce destruction, could not affect the great issue. Decision would be reached off Cadiz. If his luck changed, Nelson might yet have the chance for which he had waited, and Collingwood, his old and experienced friend, would be with him.

He followed Blackwood to London, accompanied by Emma Hamilton and his two sisters. It was not long before Emma had a note, written after an interview with Lord Barham, telling her that a message had been sent to the *Victory* by the shutter-telegraph which, on a clear day, sent messages from hill-top to hill-top to Portsmouth. She was to make ready for sea. Nelson asked Emma that everything should be prepared against his own departure.

Crowded and happy as his interlude ashore had been, Nelson could not find it in himself to refuse the request of the Government that he should once more resume his command. As it was the Mediterranean which was now threatened, it was fitting that the man who had served in that sea with such sustained credit should continue its guardian.

In the late evening of September 13th Nelson bade farewell to Emma Hamilton, to his daughter Horatia and to those of his family who remained at Merton. Once more, as so often before in his life, he took the Portsmouth road.

3

The Scene is Set

ON THE NIGHT HE LEFT HOME Nelson wrote in
his private diary: 'At half-past Ten drove from dear, dear
Merton, where I left all which I hold dear in this World, to
go to serve my King and Country. May the Great God
whom I adore enable me to fulfil the expectations of my
Country, and if it is His good pleasure that I should return,
my thanks will never cease being offered up to the Throne
of His Mercy. If it is His good providence to cut short my
days upon Earth, I bow with the greatest submission, rely-
ing that He will protect those so dear to me, that I may
leave behind. His Will be done: Amen, Amen, Amen.'

At six o'clock in the morning of Saturday, September
14th, he arrived at Portsmouth. 'Having arranged all my
business,' his diary continued, 'embarked . . . with Mr Rose
and Mr Canning at two; got on board the *Victory* at St
Helens . . . preparing for sea.' Rose was an old friend,
Canning a new one, and they were his guests at dinner.
Both men were in office, Rose as Vice-President of the
Board of Trade, Canning as Treasurer of the Navy.

It was an unforgettable moment when the boatswain
piped the admiral over the side for the last time. All had
indeed been memorable since early morning, when Nelson
made his quarters at the George Inn, conducting his affairs
from that convenient place. He took 'a by-way to the
beach' and entered his barge from a spot where bathing
machines then stood, his idea being 'to elude the populace'.
The scene as he left England as told by Southey, a contemporary, is as follows:

'. . . a crowd collected in his train, pressing forward to
obtain sight of his face: many were in tears, and many

knelt down before him, and blessed him as he passed. England has had many heroes, but never one who so entirely possessed the love of his fellow-countrymen as Nelson. All men knew that his heart was as humane as it was fearless: that there was not in his nature the slightest alloy of selfishness or cupidity; but that, with perfect and entire devotion, he served his Country with all his heart, and with all his soul, and with all his strength; and therefore they loved him as truly and as fervently as he loved England. They pressed upon the parapet to gaze after him when his barge pushed off, and he was returning their cheers by waving his hat. The sentinels, who endeavoured to prevent them from trespassing upon this ground, were wedged among the crowd; and an Officer who, not very prudently upon such an occasion, ordered them to drive the people down with their bayonets, was compelled speedily to retreat; for the people would not be debarred from gazing till the last moment upon the hero – the darling hero of England!'

There is, alas, no firm evidence for this set-piece, the local story being that Nelson was helped into his barge, off Southsea beach, by a one-legged fiddler; but it has established its place in the admiral's legend, as has the remark that he is said to have made to Hardy, his flag-captain: 'I had their huzzas before – I have their hearts now!'

As the great three-decker made her majestic way down Channel she had only the *Euryalus* in company, but that was fitting, for if the *Victory* carried the commander and genius of the fleet, Blackwood and the frigates would give it eyes.

I I

By September 16th Nelson was off Portland; next day he was off Plymouth, where he picked up the *Ajax* and *Thunderer;* and by the 23rd Cape Finisterre was in sight.

On the 25th he was off Lisbon, and on the 28th, the day before his forty-seventh birthday, he wrote in his diary: 'Nearly calm. In the evening joined the Fleet under Vice-Admiral Collingwood. Saw the Enemy's Fleet in Cadiz, amounting to thirty-five or thirty-six Sail of the Line.' He had caught up with Villeneuve at last.

He had already sent orders ahead that he was not to be accorded the usual commander-in-chief's salute of gun-fire, since this would have given immediate notice of his presence to the enemy, but his arrival was almost ecstatically welcomed. There was a double reason for this. Nelson had always been loved by those who served with him, whatever the circumstances, while it was a fact that the fleet before Cadiz was restive and bored. 'For Charity's sake, send us Lord Nelson, ye men of power!' That was the prayer of Codrington of the *Orion*, and it was echoed by Fremantle of the *Neptune* and by other officers of standing.

Nelson's command was made up of ships from diverse squadrons. There were the veteran captains who had shared the long watch off Toulon and the chase to the West Indies; there was Collingwood's flying squadron, and there were ships which had fought under Sir Robert Calder in the previous July. Others would soon arrive from home, among them Sir Edward Berry, in Nelson's famous old ship, the *Agamemnon*. There were no fewer than four flag officers besides Nelson – Vice-Admirals Collingwood and Calder; Rear-Admirals the Earl of Northesk and Louis.

Nelson had brought orders with him to recall Sir Robert Calder for the court martial arising from his summer action, for which he had himself asked, and he intended to take with him such captains as were willing to give evidence at the trial. One other admiral was about to be detached, with ships whose supplies were low, in order to water and provision at Tetuan and Gibraltar, and to convoy merchantmen through the Straits. The lot would fall upon Louis, a particular friend of Nelson's.

Of the four subordinate admirals, Collingwood was not merely the senior, he was the most experienced and distinguished. A Northumbrian, and some ten years older than his chief, he had been a close friend of Nelson's since they had served together as lieutenants in the West Indies in the seventeen-seventies. Austere, reserved, and something of a martinet, Collingwood's severe discipline had taxed the patience of the blockaders: but Collingwood was a man whom to know was to admire, and Nelson, who had long since pierced through to the essential man, loved him dearly. Not only was Collingwood a thoughtful student of war, he was as brave as a lion, as he had already shown in action under Howe at the Glorious First of June, and under Jervis at Cape St Vincent, where the gunnery of his ship, HMS *Excellent*, was the marvel of friend and foe. Collingwood knew more about the conditions of blockade service off the coast of Spain than most men, and it was well that Nelson and he were so close, or Collingwood might have chafed at the appearance of a senior admiral. But Collingwood had long since clarified his judgement of Nelson. Just four years earlier, he had written to a friend: 'Lord Nelson is an incomparable man, a blessing to any country that is engaged in such a war. His successes in most of his undertakings are the best proofs of his genius and his talents. Without much previous preparation or plan he has the faculty of discovering advantages as they arise, and the good judgement to turn them to his use. An enemy that commits a false step in his view is ruined, and it comes on him with an impetuosity that allows him no time to recover.'

Sir Robert Calder was a different type of man altogether. Socially inclined, he had many friends in the Navy, though Lady Nelson once wrote to her husband that 'his love of money is great', and the fact must always have been evident. An older man even than Collingwood, he was then sixty, and he had taken part as a midshipman in the capture of the *Hermione*, the richest prize on record. His share had been no less than £1,800. He had fought at St Vincent as Jervis's flag-captain, and was said to have shown some jealousy at Nelson's part in that encounter. He had been knighted immediately afterwards, an honour which was followed within a year by a baronetcy.

There were those who said that Calder, with prize-money in mind, had taken too much care to guard his captures after the action off Finisterre, at the expense of more important considerations. Nelson and Collingwood in fact both sympathized with him in the trial which was before him, though Nelson, kindly as he was, thought him 'too wise' to take sensible advice about the whole matter. Nelson had been ordered to send him home in a frigate, but with extraordinary generosity, which may well have been misguided but which certainly showed no lack of feeling, he disobeyed, and allowed Calder to stay in his splendid three-decker, the *Prince of Wales*, until another ship of comparable size arrived from England, and then to sail back in her.

If, in Nelson, the decision was generous, it was shocking in Calder even to have contemplated allowing the fleet to be weakened by such a powerful unit, and that solely on account of *amour propre*. Nelson had urged Sir Robert to stay with him a few days longer, being convinced that the enemy would soon make their sortie, since the season was advanced. Calder did not agree, and indeed he did not hold his opinion alone, for Fremantle and others took much the same view. So in due time he sailed home, running the not inconsiderable risk of being engaged and captured by the Rochefort squadron, whose whereabouts was then uncertain. And what he next did should have robbed him of every particle of sympathy. 'What do you think of Calder's modesty,' wrote Collingwood to his sister, after Trafalgar had been fought and won. 'The first thing he did on his arrival at Portsmouth was to write to me signifying his claim to *share*. There was a great indelicacy in it under all circumstances, and not a little portion of ignorance.' Calder's astounding claim was a 'share' in the prize-money which he knew would accrue from Nelson's victory. Never was kindness more greedily betrayed.

When Calder had departed, Rear-Admiral the Earl of Northesk became third in command. He was a Scot, and the son of a sailor. He had learnt his seamanship under Rodney, and was a few months older than Nelson, though he had no opportunity, during his service life, to distinguish himself in a general action. His flag-ship was the *Britannia*, the oldest and one of the largest units in the fleet, but she was a slow sailer, and it was only Lord Northesk's determined handling which enabled her to take an active part in the battle. Neither Nelson nor Collingwood seem to have known Northesk at all well, but they soon came to a sound understanding, and made up an harmonious chain of command.

Nelson's methods differed radically from those of Collingwood. He worked by frankness and confidence. 'The reception I met with on joining the fleet,' he wrote, 'caused the sweetest sensation of my life.' Greeting old acquaintances with infectious warmth, he soon made it his business to get to know and to enthuse everyone who had not served with him before. And then there was his 'Plan' to unfold. 'I believe my arrival was most welcome not only to the commander of the Fleet,' he wrote to Emma Hamilton, 'but also to every individual in it; and when I came to explain to them the "Nelson touch" it was like an electric shock. Some shed tears, all approved. – "It was new – it was singular – it was simple!" and, from Admirals downwards, it was repeated – "It must succeed, if ever they will allow us to get at them! You are, my Lord, surrounded by friends whom you inspire with confidence." ' 'As soon as these emotions were past,' he told another correspondent, 'I laid before them the Plan I had previously arranged for attacking the Enemy, and it was not only my pleasure to find it generally approved but clearly perceived and understood.' The Plan thus referred to, and spoken of as 'the Nelson touch', was afterwards formally issued to the captains as a Secret Memorandum, which is one of the classic documents of its kind. Its essence had already been conveyed to Captain Keats of the *Superb*, in a conversation which he recorded as follows:

'One day, walking with Lord Nelson in the grounds at Merton, talking on naval matters, he said to me: "No day can be long enough to arrange a couple of fleets and fight a decisive battle, according to the old system. When *we* meet them (I was to have been with him), for meet them we shall, I'll tell you how I shall fight them. I shall form the Fleet into three Divisions in three Lines. One Division shall be composed of twelve or fourteen of the fastest two-decked ships, which I shall always keep to windward, or in a situation of advantage; and I shall put them under an Officer who, I am sure, will employ them in the manner I wish, if possible. I consider it will always be in my power to throw them into Battle in any part I may choose; but if circumstances prevent their being carried against the Enemy where I desire, I shall feel certain he will employ them effectually, and perhaps in a more advantageous manner than if he could have followed my orders.

' "With the remaining part of the Fleet formed in two lines, I shall go at them at once, if I can, about one-third of their line from their leading Ship." He then said, "What do you think of it?" Such a question I felt required consideration. I paused. Seeing it, he said: "But I'll tell you what *I* think of it. I think it will surprise and confound the Enemy. They won't know what I am about. It will bring forward a pell-mell Battle, and that is what I want." '

Thinking it almost impossible to bring
a fleet of forty Sail of the Line into a
Line of Battle in variable Winds thick
weather and other circumstances which
must occur, without such a loss of
time that the opportunity would
probably be lost of bringing the
Enemy to Battle in such a manner
as to make the business decisive—

I have therefore made up my mind to
keep the fleet in that position of
Sailing (with the exception of the first
and Second in Command) that the order
of Sailing is to be the order of Battle,
placing the fleet in two Lines of Sixteen
Ships each with an advanced Squadron

The 'Fighting Memorandum'

The Secret Memorandum, though more elaborate, expressed exactly the same idea, though in action it was seriously modified by the fact that Nelson had under his command a smaller force than he had assumed, and had therefore to make his attack in two columns, not three. The main features were as follows. 'The Order of Sailing is to be the Order of Battle.' 'The Second in Command will, after my intentions are made known to him, have the entire direction of his Line to make the attack upon the Enemy, and to follow up the blow until they are captured or destroyed.' 'Something must be left to chance; nothing is sure in a Sea Fight beyond all others. Shot will carry away the masts and yards of friends as well as foes; but I look with confidence to a Victory before the Van of the Enemy could succour their Rear.' Perhaps the most memorable sentence was an echo of Lord Hawke, whose fighting tradition Nelson had inherited: '... In case Signals can neither be seen or perfectly understood, no Captain can do very wrong if he places his Ship alongside that of an Enemy.'

It may seem surprising that a document so apparently simple should have appeared with the effect of an 'electric shock' to veteran captains; but they, like their enemies the French and Spaniards, had been brought up in a rigid and formal school of tactics, one which had been built up, over the centuries, with the object of strengthening mutual confidence. Nelson, who gave his captains just such confidence, soon taught them to believe that mutual support was given best by getting alongside the enemy rather than by keeping station in a line of bearing.

Writing on October 9th to Collingwood, Nelson said:

'I send you my Plan of Attack, as far as a man dare venture to guess at the very uncertain position the Enemy may be found in. But, my dear friend, it is to place you perfectly at ease respecting my intentions, and to give full scope to your judgement for carrying them into effect. We can, my dear Coll, have no little jealousies. We have only one great object in view, that of annihilating our Enemies, and getting a glorious Peace for our Country. No man has more confidence in another than I have in you: and no man will render your services more justice than your very old friend NELSON AND BRONTË.'

III

While Nelson was infusing the watching fleet with his own gay confidence, what of the enemy, apparently impregnable and snug in Cadiz?

The Combined Fleet had reached the southern port by August 21st, to find itself little better off than at Ferrol. Cadiz, together with the surrounding countryside, had not recovered from an epidemic which had ravaged half Andalusia. There was little food; dockyard supplies were inadequate for a large force; and the ill-feeling which at the best of times was active, beneath the surface, between the navies of France and Spain had been roused by the fact that both ships which Calder had captured in July had been Spanish. Their comrades-in-arms believed them to have been 'deserted in action and sacrificed' by their Allies, and although there was no adequate reason for this view, it did nothing to ease an always tricky relationship. At first Villeneuve was actually refused supplies, and it took a peremptory order from Madrid before he could get his essential stores. Even so, the authorities of the port greatly disliked having to accept French paper money, or drafts on Paris. In view of the financial reputation of the French Government, this was not surprising.

The personalities of the leaders of the Combined Fleet were as strongly contrasted as those of their opponents. Admiral Pierre de Villeneuve himself was a Provençal of aristocratic lineage. Like many of his kind who were prepared to serve the Revolutionary Government, he had been given quick promotion. He was a rear-admiral by the age of thirty-three, and at the time of Trafalgar was actually some years younger than Nelson, who had himself attained a flag rank before the age of forty. Villeneuve, like his colleague and friend Decrès, had been a pupil of Suffren, the greatest tactician the French Navy produced. Suffren's five engagements in the East Indies against Sir Edward Hughes were among the most stubborn ever fought, and were a fine school of discipline for a young officer.

The French second-in-command, Rear-Admiral Dumanoir le Pelley, was even younger than his chief. Thirty-five years old, he too had worn the King's uniform in the time of the old regime, and, again like Villeneuve, he was of an aristocratic family. So was Magon, the next in command, who had had more battle experience than most of his fellow officers. A Breton, he had fought off Ushant against Keppel, and in the West Indies against Rodney, and he had experienced a spell as a prisoner of war in England. One of Napoleon's entourage, who knew all the commanders concerned, gave it as his view that had Magon been in Villeneuve's place the Emperor's orders would have been obeyed, and the invasion of Britain attempted. He was impetuous and daring, and possessed all the certainty and assurance which Villeneuve lacked.

Of the French captains, Cosmao, another Breton, was the most outstanding, and his ship, the *Pluton*, was one of the best-manned in the fleet. It was Cosmao who had taken Diamond Rock, and he had saved at least one Spanish ship in Calder's action. Infernet of the *Intrépide* was another able officer, though his ship was an indifferent sailer. Gourrège of the *Aigle* and Maistral of the *Neptune* were also dependable. Villeneuve spoke of Maistral as 'a pattern to the fleet'. Gourrège was a rough-and-ready Breton merchant skipper brought into the navy by the Revolution; Maistral was yet another survivor from the older service.

Other good captains were Lucas of the *Redoutable*, a man of humble origin, but one whose pupilage derived from Suffren, and Baudoin of the *Fougueux*.

As for the Spanish officers, they had both advantages and handicaps as compared with their Allies. By and large they were older men, and their service had not suffered political disruption, at any rate on the scale of the French Revolution, but their sea experience had been more limited and, on the whole, less varied. Neither the French nor the Spanish had any living tradition of successful fleet encounter, which was in fact the gravest disadvantage under which any such a body as theirs could labour. If they were not beaten before they put to sea, yet even their bellicose Emperor did not envisage that they could cope with odds, which to the British seaman gave a spice to any fight.

Don Federico Gravina, the senior Spanish flag-officer, had been a sailor since boyhood. At forty-nine he was one of the most respected man in his country's service. He had been anxious not to continue under Villeneuve, but had been persuaded by his Government to remain in his command, at any rate until the immediate crisis had been resolved. His war experience went back to the days of the great Siege of Gibraltar, and he had been second-in-command of the fleet which had co-operated with Hood at Toulon, at the opening of the Revolutionary War, before his country had changed sides.

Vice-Admiral Alava, or D'Alava, second in the Spanish hierarchy, was three years older than Gravina, with whom he had served in earlier days at Gibraltar. Supporting these senior officers were Rear-Admiral Cisneros, who had taken part at the Battle of Cape St Vincent; Rear-Admiral Escano; Commodore Churruca of the *San Juan Nepomuceno*, a highly intelligent tactician who had no opinion of his French commander-in-chief; Commodore Galiano, and Valdez of the *Neptuno*. Valdez, who was not yet thirty-five, was one of the most popular officers in the Spanish service, for it was he who, more than any other, had been responsible for saving the towering *Santissima Trinidad* from capture off Cape St Vincent, on that memorable day in 1797 when Nelson had won a Knighthood of the Bath.

One of Gravina's captains was an Irishman, carrying on a well-established tradition of employment in the armed forces of Continental countries. He went by the name of Don Enrique Macdonell, and was in command of the three-decker *Rayo*. He too had served the Spaniards at the siege of Gibraltar, in the Regimento de Hibernia, a corps originally raised among Jacobite refugees to Spain three-quarters of a century earlier. Transferring later to the navy, he had actually retired, but on hearing of Gravina's desperate need for trained officers had volunteered his services. As the *Victory*, together with many other British ships, had French names in her muster-book through most of the Napoleonic War, a mixture of nationalities was not in the least uncommon in navies where men were always hard to get.

IV

At the end of September, when Nelson arrived off Cape St Vincent, Napoleon, having abandoned his invasion, solved the problem of how to induce the combined fleet to leave Cadiz by ordering it to sail forthwith to Naples, and thence, after landing troops for employment in Italy, back to Toulon. He still believed that his strategy had scattered the British, and that the force outside Cadiz was not a strong one.

The orders which he issued on October 18th through Decrès gave the French admiral discretion not to risk a battle unless circumstances were favourable, but although the Emperor knew, as early as September 20th, that the blockaders had been reinforced, he left Paris three days later for his land campaign without modifying his orders.

Thus, almost carelessly, did he throw away his fleet.

On hearing the Emperor's wishes, Gravina went on board Villeneuve's flagship and announced that fourteen of his ships were almost ready for sea. Soldiers had been ordered to fill the deficiency in sailors. On the same evening, signal stations on the coast reported that a three-decker and two 74-gun ships were joining Collingwood from the westward. It was not then known that it was Nelson himself who had arrived, but the addition of strength caused Villeneuve uneasiness.

The embarkation of troops for service in Italy was completed by October 2nd, but on the evening of that day Gravina had news from Lisbon which gave everyone disquiet. It was said that Nelson had indeed arrived, 'with four of the line and great projects for attacking, bombarding and burning the Combined Squadron'. The effect was startling: the news itself was only too likely to be true, and a defence flotilla was hastily organized consisting of gunboats, bomb-vessels and other small craft, manned by officers and men from the fleet. And now, instead of being able to get the ships of the line into the Bay as and when they were ready, the fear of an impetuous attack, such as Nelson had made on Boulogne, kept them crowded in the harbour out of harm's way. But despite the alarm, Villeneuve continued to proclaim his intention of sailing the moment he had a fair wind.

At Cadiz, in fine autumn weather, there is often a land breeze at night from the east, favourable for ships to leave the harbour. Outside, in the morning, a westerly wind is usually fair for a run to the Mediterranean. On the evening of October 7th an easterly breeze sprang up, and the signal was made to prepare to weigh. It was quickly annulled, for the wind increased to such an extent as to threaten to carry the ships, once they were in the Bay, 'diametrically contrary to the course they had to make', in Villeneuve's own words. In fact, he had been increasingly affected not

only by his pervading fear of Nelson, but by the new disposition of the blockading force. Nelson's custom differed
from that of Collingwood, who believed in visibility. Nelson withdrew his main fleet right out of sight, some leagues
into the Atlantic, leaving only the watching frigates inshore, with a communicating squadron of fast ships of the
line, few of which were ever simultaneously in sight from
the Spanish signal stations. Nelson might be there, but in
what his strength consisted, and how it would be exercised,
no one could be certain.

Villeneuve's next act was to summon a Council of War.
Nelson used to say that a Council of War always voted for
doing nothing, which showed an acute reading of history.
The French and Spanish officers met aboard the *Bucentaure* on October 8th. Seven French and seven Spanish
commanders were present: Villeneuve had his two flag
officers, Dumanoir and Magon, together with Captains
Cosmao, Maistral, Lavillegris of the *Mont Blanc*, and
Prigny, who acted as Chief of Staff. Gravina brought with
him Admirals Alava, Escano and Cisneros, and three
commodores, Galiano, Macdonell and Hore.

The Spaniards had come to the meeting with a prepared
and unanimous opinion. After Villeneuve had told them his
orders, they rose one by one to dissent from the view that
they should sail at once. Delay, they argued, was in their
favour, for the British could hardly remain much longer
where they were, if only for lack of supplies. Moreover the
new levies badly wanted a few weeks of further training.
When they had all spoken, Prigny urged the same opinion
as the Spaniards. 'They,' he said of the British, 'have kept
the seas without intermission since 1793, while most of our
fleet have scarcely weighed anchor for eight years.' Prigny
favoured the employment of the defence flotilla, and suggested that no orders could bind them to attempt the impossible.

Such words from a fellow-Frenchman were too much for

Magon, who not only roundly contradicted his colleague, but used some expressions which wounded Spanish honour. His speech caused a scene, and Commodore Galiano, his hand on his sword-hilt, seemed about to challenge Magon to a duel. Villeneuve calmed things down for a while, but even he was not at his most tactful in dealing with his allies. This time Gravina himself took up the cudgels, and said that only a madman would think of sailing in the present circumstances.

'Do you not see, sir,' he said to Villeneuve, 'that the barometer is falling?' 'It is not the glass, but the courage of certain persons that is falling,' replied the French commander-in-chief. The sneer was too much for the courtly Gravina. 'Admiral,' he said, and looked Villeneuve straight in the face, 'whenever the Spanish fleet has gone into action side by side with allies, it has ever borne its part valiantly, and led the way, the foremost under fire. This, as you must admit, we fully proved at the battle off Finisterre.'

The Council ended with the customary formal vote. The result was a decision 'to await the favourable opportunity ... which may arise from bad weather that would drive the enemy away from these waters, or from the necessity which he will experience of dividing the force of his squadron in order to protect his trade in the Mediterranean and the convoys that may be threatened by the Squadrons from Cartagena and from Toulon. . . .'

As the Minutes of the Council would be scrutinized in Paris, they ended: 'The Admirals concluded ... by renewing the orders to be in readiness to weigh, so as to be able to set sail at the first signal without losing a single instant.'

Nelson had not been far wrong in his view of such conferences.

v

While the Allies were in Council at Cadiz, reinforcements were gradually reaching Nelson. On October 7th the *Defiance* joined from Portsmouth, and the *Amphion* frigate from Lisbon. The *Amphion*'s captain was William Hoste, one of Nelson's favourite pupils. Hoste had been with his chief as early as 1793, and had served in several of his battles. The *Amphion* had to be detached shortly before Trafalgar for service in the Mediterranean, and the order nearly broke Hoste's heart. He felt he would miss the fight, and so he did.

By contrast, the captain of the *Defiance*, Philip Durham, was one of the luckiest men in the navy. He had been trained under Howe, had served in battle with Rodney, had survived the foundering of the *Royal George* at Spithead, fought in Calder's action, and been just in time to catch Nelson on one of his flying visits to the Admiralty. The pair met in a waiting-room. Nelson said: 'I am just appointed to the Mediterranean command, and sail immediately; I am sorry your ship is not ready, I should have been very glad to have you.'

Durham answered: 'Ask Lord Barham to place me under your Lordship's orders, and I will soon be ready.' Nelson did so, and left Durham the necessary orders at Portsmouth.

When the *Defiance* joined the fleet Durham brought out 750,000 dollars with him, for the garrison at Minorca. On paying his respects Nelson said: 'Durham, I am glad to see you, but your stay will be short, for Sir Robert Calder sails tomorrow and takes with him all the captains who were in his action, to give evidence at the court martial.' He added: 'The wind is at north-east, and the enemy will soon be out.' It was like turning a knife in the wound.

But when Durham went on board the *Prince of Wales*, Calder's ship, he found that the order to the captains was permissive. They were to go home 'if willing'. Durham was not. He longed to see action under Nelson, which was the wish of every active officer, and he did not love Sir Robert Calder, who owed his first sighting of the Combined Fleet to the alertness of the *Defiance*, but who gave the ship no special credit in his dispatch. Moreover, Durham sent some signals to Sir Robert next day which the admiral was pleased to term 'over-zealous', and altogether Durham was glad of a change of command.

Nelson forgot about the dollars, and when Durham sought to remind him jocularly said: 'If the Spaniards come out, fire them at them, and pay them back in their own coin!' In fact, they were sent in to Gibraltar just before the action.

On October 8th the *Royal Sovereign* reported, as did the *Naiad* frigate from Gibraltar. The *Royal Sovereign* was an important addition of strength. Nelson knew her quality of old. A splendid three-decker, she had fought with Howe at the Glorious First of June, eleven years earlier, and had taken part in the watch on Toulon. Newly coppered and repaired, she was a heartening sight.

Collingwood, who was flying his flag in the *Dreadnought*, soon transferred to her, at first with some misgiving, but with increasing pleasure as he grew to learn the ship's qualities. The change was to have two consequences in battle: the first was that, as was the case with the *Victory*, Collingwood's ship out-sailed the rest of his line; the second was that the *Dreadnought*, though a slow sailer, had been so well exercised in gunnery by Collingwood that, when she was at last able to join the *mêlée*, her fire-power was exceptional, even for her large size. The appearance of the *Royal Sovereign* enabled Nelson to send Calder home in the *Prince of Wales*.

Rear-Admiral Louis had been detached, on October 2nd, to Gibraltar and Tetuan for water and provisions, and had taken with him the *Queen*, the *Canopus*, *Spencer*, *Zealous* and *Tigre* – tried ships, all but the first of which had been with Nelson on his chase to the West Indies. The *Donegal*, another veteran, followed them on October 17th. Louis, like Hoste, had been regretful at the order, but Nelson did not expect the enemy to come out until after Louis had rejoined. He detached these particular ships first, so that they should have every chance of being there at the day of battle. No one knew their quality better than Nelson.

On October 13th the *Agamemnon*, Captain Sir Edward Berry, arrived from England, and made no little stir in the fleet. 'When she was signalled,' so a contemporary reported, 'Nelson exclaimed with glee: "Here comes Berry! *Now* we shall have a battle!"' Both ship and captain recalled much in Nelson's life. Between 1793 and 1796 Nelson had made his name, as a Mediterranean man, in the *Agamemnon*, while Sir Edward Berry had been his flag-captain at the Nile, and had served with him earlier still, at Cape St Vincent. He had been foremost in Nelson's boarding-party in that battle. Afterwards, at Court, when George III had remarked on the loss of Nelson's right arm, Nelson had answered at once by presenting his 'right hand', Berry, to his Sovereign.

Berry was indeed the stormy petrel of the Navy. He had already been in several general actions, and was to survive two more. He had left England on October 2nd, and, when eight days out, had been chased and all but taken by Allemand's powerful detachment. Berry had then had one of the narrowest shaves of his life.

On October 14th the *Africa*, which, like the *Agamemnon*, was a 64-gun ship, joined from home, and the Trafalgar fleet was complete. On the same day Blackwood in the *Euryalus* signalled that the Combined Fleet was at the harbour's mouth. Nelson now placed the *Defence* and *Agamemnon* 'from seven to ten leagues west of Cadiz', and the *Mars* and *Colossus* 'five leagues east of the fleet', adding: 'by this chain I hope to have a constant communication with the Frigates off Cadiz'.

Nelson's use of the *Mars* for this special service delighted her Scots captain, George Duff, who had not met Nelson earlier in his career. Duff was a favourite with Collingwood, and had a smart ship. He had a kinsman of the same name acting as his first lieutenant, and a son of thirteen, called Norwich, among his 'younkers'. His letters to his wife illustrate the commander-in-chief's effect on such a man. He wrote on October 1st: 'I dined with his Lordship yesterday, and had a very merry dinner. He certainly is the pleasantest Admiral I ever served under.' Nine days later he said: 'He is so good and pleasant a man, that we all wish to do what he likes, without any kind of orders. I have been myself very lucky with most of my Admirals, but I really think the present the pleasantest I have ever met with: even this little detachment is a kind thing to me, there being so many senior Officers to me in the Fleet, as it shows his attention, and wish to bring me forward; but I believe I have to thank my old friend Collingwood for it, as he was on board the *Victory* when I was sent for.' And three days before Trafalgar: 'You ask me about Lord Nelson, and how I like him. I have already answered that question as every person must do that ever served under him.' The later story of Duff and his ship belongs, appropriately enough in view of her name, to the battle itself.

A few days before the enemy engaged, Nelson became worried about Hardy. The flag-captain's health was poorly, and he was forced for a time to keep to his cabin, Nelson at times refusing to eat, now that the friend who usually did this service for him was not there to cut up his meat.

When Hardy recovered he asked Nelson if the *Victory* might spend a night away from the fleet, repairing sails. The request was at first refused, but later granted, Nelson realizing that it would make a difference to the speed of the ship in action. But the admiral was sleepless all the time the repairs were being done, and when Beatty asked him in the morning how his head was, Nelson having complained of pains, he snapped: 'Heads and tails be damned! I care nothing about them. I wish we were back with the fleet.'

Very soon, they were.

VI

By the time of the issue of his orders of September 18th for the Combined Fleet to proceed to the Mediterranean, Napoleon had decided to replace Villeneuve by Admiral Rosily. In its way, this was a desperate step, for although Rosily was at the head of the vice-admirals' list, he had not served afloat for many years, having been engaged in purely administrative posts. Decrès at first hesitated to tell his old friend the Emperor's decision in plain terms, and when he heard rumours of a change in command, Villeneuve hoped that he would be allowed to act as Rosily's second.

On October 12th, four days after the Council of War, Rosily reached Madrid. The Spanish posting system had broken down, and the roads beyond Cordova were infested with brigands. Rosily was advised by the French ambassador not to proceed on his way until arrangements had been made for him to travel in safety. It was a ten days' journey from Madrid to Cadiz, but in half that time Villeneuve, already unhappy both at his prospects in battle and at the deliberations of his Council, had learnt of his successor's advent, and had guessed that he had lost the Emperor's favour.

On October 18th, without saying a word to anyone, Villeneuve suddenly ordered Magon to sea with seven of the line and a frigate. Magon was to try to capture Blackwood's squadron, and to find out the strength behind it. But before the order could be carried into effect, Villeneuve had news by telegraph of Louis' appearance at Gibraltar, where there were already two British ships of the line. Villeneuve's natural inference was that Nelson must be in the weakest relative position he would ever be likely to find him. The combination of news was decisive. He gave orders for the Fleet to prepare to weigh anchor.

'Enemy have their topsail yards hoisted.' The news came from the frigate *Sirius* early in the morning on October 19th. An hour later word came: 'The enemy ships are coming out of port or getting under sail.' In ten minutes Blackwood passed it out to the *Phoebe*, which he kept to the westward. As the light strengthened, they got the message through to the *Mars*, and by half-past nine Nelson himself had it. The *Victory* was then nearly fifty miles to the westward of Cadiz. Without waiting to form order of sailing, he signalled: 'General chase, south-east', and shortly afterwards made the signal to prepare for battle. His course was for the Straits of Gibraltar.

What had in fact happened to the enemy was that Magon, with nine of the line and three frigates, had cleared the entrance to Cadiz by seven o'clock in the morning, when the wind suddenly dropped. Blackwood instantly sent a sloop to Gibraltar to warn Louis. Magon's ships lay becalmed until the early afternoon, when a breeze sprang up from west-north-west. They then stood to the northward, shadowed by the *Euryalus* and *Sirius*, while the *Phoebe* and *Naiad* kept touch with the *Defence*, which was ten miles to the westward and in touch with other ships. Owing to the delay in getting out of the harbour, any hope the French had had of finding the British scattered had disappeared. There was no chance of capturing the ever-alert Blackwood, and as the wind in the bay was still southerly, Magon could not get in again. Villeneuve decided that he now had no choice but to sail the whole fleet.

While the enemy were in process of coming out, men of the British Fleet remembered those at home.

'What think you, my own dearest love?' wrote Blackwood to his wife. 'At this moment the Enemy are coming out, and as if determined to have a fair fight; all night they had been making signals, and the morning showed them to us getting under sail. They have thirty-four sail of the line, and five Frigates. Lord Nelson, I am sorry to say, has but twenty-seven Sail of the Line with him; the rest are at Gibraltar, getting water. Not that he has not enough to bring them to close Action; but I want him to have so many as to make the most decisive battle of it that ever was, which will bring us a lasting Peace, I hope, and some prize-money. Within two hours, though our Fleet was at sixteen leagues off, I have let Lord N. know of their coming out, and I have been enabled to send a vessel off to Gibraltar, which will bring Admiral Louis and the ships in there out.'

Blackwood's message in fact arrived too late to bring Louis back in time. He was already some distance into the Mediterranean, covering the passage of supply-ships for Craig. The letter continued:

'. . . At this moment we are within four miles of the Enemy, and talking to Lord Nelson by means of Sir H. Popham's signals, though so distant, but repeated along by the rest of the Frigates of this Squadron. You see also, my Harriet, I have time to write to you, and to assure you that to the last moment of my breath, I shall be as much attached to you as man can be, which I am sure you will credit. It is very odd how I have been dreaming all night of my carrying home despatches. God send so much good luck! The day is fine; the sight, of course, beautiful. I expect, before this hour tomorrow, to have carried General Decrès on board the *Victory* in my barge, which I have just been painting. God bless you. No more at present.'

The writer had heard the rumour of a change in the command of the Combined Fleet, and had assumed that it was Napoleon's Minister of Marine who was to replace Villeneuve.

As for Nelson, as soon as Blackwood had conveyed his momentous tidings by means of Sir Home Popham's newly issued and improved signal-book, he wrote to Emma Hamilton as follows:

> '*Victory*, October 19, 1805, Noon. Cadiz, E.S.E.
> 16 Leagues.
>
> 'My dearest Beloved Emma, the dear Friend of my Bosom, the Signal has been made that the Enemy's Combined Fleet are coming out of Port. We have very little wind, so that I have no hopes of seeing them before tomorrow. May the God of Battles crown my endeavours with success; at all events, I will take care that my name shall ever be most dear to you and Horatia, both of whom I love as much as my own life. And as my last writing before the Battle will be to you, so I hope in God that I shall live to finish my letter after the Battle. May Heaven bless you prays your
> *Nelson and Brontë.*'

As darkness fell on October 19th he wrote in his private diary: 'Directed the Fleet to observe my motions during the night, and for *Britannia*, *Prince* and *Dreadnought*, they being heavy sailers, to take their stations as convenient; and for *Mars*, *Orion*, *Belleisle*, *Leviathan*, *Bellerophon* and *Polyphemus* to go ahead during the night, and to carry a light, standing for the Strait's Mouth.'

Next day, Nelson added a paragraph to his letter.

'October 20th – In the morning we were close to the Mouth of the Streights, but the wind had not come far enough to the Westward to allow the Combined Fleets to weather the Shoals off Trafalgar; but they were counted as far as forty Sail of Ships of War, which I suppose to be 34 of the Line, and six Frigates. A group of them was seen off the Lighthouse of Cadiz this morning, but it blows so very fresh and thick weather, that I rather believe they will go into the Harbour before night. May God Almighty give us success over these fellows, and enable us to get a Peace. . . .'

These were the last words he ever wrote to the woman he loved. He also sent a short note to Horatia, telling her he was sure of her prayers for his safety, conquest 'and speedy return to dear Merton and our dearest good Lady Hamilton'.

'I have not a thought except on you and the French fleet,' he had written to Emma Hamilton earlier in his command. 'All my thoughts, plans and toils tend to those two objects, and I will embrace them both so close when I can lay hold of either one or the other, that the Devil himself should not separate us.' Such dedication deserved its reward.

VII

October 20th, which was a Sunday, was no day of rest: it was one of manoeuvre, though in any fleet commanded by Nelson religious observance would have been as usual.

In the early morning there was a light wind from southward, and this enabled Villeneuve to get his fleet to sea without confusion. By about seven o'clock all the Allied ships had left Cadiz, and at first stood to the westward. As they cleared the bay, the wind began to freshen, with strong gusts and heavy rain. Some of the Spaniards split their topsails in reefing, and fell away to leeward.

The *Sirius*, which had given the earliest news of enemy activity, intercepted an American vessel, and found that she was out of Belfast, bound for Gibraltar. While the boarding party were still away, the frigate came under fire from a distant broadside, which might be considered as the first shots at Trafalgar. A little later the *Sirius* saw the same French battleship which had fired at her send over a party of investigation. The American was the only neutral recorded to have seen the preliminaries to battle.

Daylight was scarcely clear when the *Euryalus*, ever alert, reported Sir Edward Berry in a typical incident. The *Agamemnon*, with a brig in tow, was standing, apparently unconscious of her danger, straight for the enemy. 'Made the signal to the *Agamemnon*,' noted the master of the frigate in his log. 'Repeated it with many guns before it was noticed.' Captain Blackwood, having at last held Berry's attention, ordered him to repeat the Allied numbers to Nelson.

At eight o'clock, while at the mouth of the Straits and still hoping to meet with Louis, Nelson ordered the *Victory* to be hove-to. Shortly afterwards Collingwood, together with the captains of the *Mars, Colossus* and *Defence*, came on board and conferred with the commander-in-chief for about an hour. These captains, Duff, Morris and Hope, were ordered to keep in touch with the frigates, supporting them whenever necessary, and affording a reliable chain of communication.

'In the afternoon,' wrote Nelson in his private diary, 'Captain Blackwood telegraphed that the Enemy seemed determined to go to the westward, and that they shall *not* do if in the power of Nelson and Brontë to prevent them. At 5 telegraphed Captain B. that I relied upon his keeping sight of the Enemy.' Bruce, the *Euryalus*'s signal midshipman, and Soper, the signal hand, would have no rest till the fleets were in contact, and very little then.

While Nelson had been cruising out of Villeneuve's sight, Blackwood had seen the Allied commander-in-chief make the signal for his fleet to form order of sailing in three columns, his apparent intention being to make enough westing to ensure, later, a quick passage through the Straits by a change of course. Admiral Gravina took station to windward, he being in command of the Squadron of Observation. His duty was to keep the British frigates at a distance, and to discover the numbers and movements of Nelson's fleet, of the composition and formation of which Villeneuve was still unsure.

At about four o'clock the weather cleared, and the wind flew round to west, taking the Combined Fleet aback, and throwing it into disorder. Villeneuve signalled a new course for his columns – south-south-west – and as darkness fell, the ships were still trying to take up their new stations. At half-past seven, signalling with flares, rockets and gunfire was seen and heard ahead, and at half-past eight the brig *Argus* came under the flagship's stern and her captain hailed that, some two hours earlier, the *Achille* had sighted eighteen British ships of the line in the direction of the Straits.

Fearing to be caught in an order of sailing in which only one of three squadrons could fire without risk to friends, Villeneuve made the signal to form a single line of battle on the leewardmost ship, without regard to sequence. It was the simplest direction he could have given, under the circumstances, but it led to further confusion. The ships to leeward omitted to hoist the distinguishing lights which they should have shown, and each took station as best she could. The squadrons became mixed together, and the duller sailers dropped astern. By daylight, no true line of battle had been evolved, though the Allied fleet was beginning to assume the appearance of what Collingwood was afterwards to describe as 'a curve, convexing to leeward'.

Nelson, meanwhile, continued to close the enemy, but signalled that the Fleet would come to the wind on the starboard tack at the close of day: in effect, this was marking time. The action placed the British some ten miles to windward and some five miles in advance of the enemy during the hours of darkness, ready to act upon any move-

ment the frigates might report, and, if the wind held, ready
to force an action when daylight discovered the disposition
of the enemy. Nelson does not seem to have contemplated a
night action, and he knew that if he waited, the farther the
Combined Fleet would move from Cadiz, and the more
difficult it would be for Villeneuve to make good a retreat
to his port of refuge.

At four in the morning, Nelson ordered his fleet to stand
north by east. The movement placed him, at daylight, nine
miles directly to windward of his opponent. Just before six
o'clock, it was light enough to see the Combined Fleet sil-
houetted against the dawn.

Sailor (1807)

4

The Battle

NELSON MAY BE HELD to have been lucky in one respect: he had always realized exactly what he was fighting for, and why he lived and might die in the nation's service. When he wrote 'King ... Country ... Enemy ...' he saw precisely what he wrote: the actual George III; the Norfolk fields; and men whose political principles he detested.

He was indeed happier than those, of his own and other times, who have died in battle without the solace of knowing an adequate reason for their fate, beyond the fact that they had no choice in the matter, that it was 'the done thing', a convention to which a friendly company subscribed, and that it took nearly as much courage to reject it as to conform.

Henry V was one of Nelson's favourite plays. How often must he have pondered that scene on the field before Agincourt where Henry, disguised, talks with his soldiers, and hears a little of the plain truth about causes and consequences which, so far as men of power are concerned, is seldom so thrustingly brought home.

Nelson knew that all sane men feared death, feared wounds and pain, feared dishonour, and that it was by an outward *appearance* of courage that morale was sustained, discipline supported, self-conquest ensured. That was why, in battle itself, his exertions redoubled, and why he seemed to all around him his fullest self. It had been so at the Nile and at Copenhagen: it was so now. We have been fortunate in examples of the quality in our own time, shown under circumstances which might have daunted even Nelson, though he would not have allowed the fact to appear.

At Trafalgar, though numerically the odds were somewhat against him, Nelson went into battle with the most
complete assurance of victory in all his crowded life. Close
knowledge of conditions in the opposing fleet could in fact
only have reassured him still further, but if the enemy
stood boldly up to his advance, it was inevitable that victory must be won at high cost.

The details of October 21st are established by abundant
evidence. Villeneuve was directly between the British fleet
and Cape Trafalgar, which was about twenty-one miles
east of the *Victory*. Soon after daylight, Nelson made four
general signals. The first was to form order of sailing in
two columns. The second and fourth gave the course. The
third was to 'Prepare for Battle'. He then summoned the
captains of his four frigates, his friends Blackwood of the
Euryalus, Dundas of the *Naiad*, Capel of the *Phoebe*, who
had been with him at the Nile, and Prowse of the *Sirius* –
and it is not untypical of the change in the pace of warfare
that, with a light wind, nearly six hours elapsed after the
opposing fleets had come into visual contact, before battle
was fairly joined, and that there was leisure in those hours
to do much.

Nelson had three anxieties. The first was lest the enemy,
when they discerned his numbers, should at once turn away
and make for Cadiz. The second was the wind. It was uncertain, not more than sufficed to carry the ships over the
Atlantic swell at a walking pace, which in the case of the
indifferent sailers was more like a crawl. The third was the
limit of daylight. It was autumn, and the fight could
scarcely be general until noon, perhaps not then. That left
all too few hours to complete the business he intended.

Nelson had expressed a general view of his responsi-
bilities in a memorandum he had prepared during the chase
to the West Indies.

'The business of an English Commander-in-Chief

being first to bring the Enemy's fleet to battle on the most advantageous terms to himself (I mean that of laying his ships well on board the Enemy as expeditiously as possible), and secondly to continue them there without separating until the business is decided ... if the two fleets are both willing to fight, but little manoeuvring is necessary; the less the better: a day is soon lost in that business. ...'

It was in fact time for which he was striving – time for his pell-mell battle, and if the plan which he had circulated to his captains had to be sacrificed in some of its details in order to engage quickly, Nelson would not hesitate, whatever the risks to the leading ships. On the day, they 'scrambled into battle as soon as they could'.

The tactics of Trafalgar have led to countless arguments and much disagreement. What were Nelson's intentions? How far were they carried out? Where and why did he depart from his plan? Were his actions best under the circumstances? Could they serve as a model for the future conduct of operations?

Some of these questions cannot now be answered completely, since Nelson did not live to write his own account of the battle, but to most of them there is a reasonable reply. His intention was victory, and it was achieved. The principal element in his plan, attack in column, was in fact carried out, and it was unquestionably the best in the circumstances since, if the enemy stood his ground, it ensured decision, while if he did not, conditions of chase – to which it could be adapted – would apply. But to elevate the tactics of Trafalgar to the status of a doctrine is carrying the matter too far, as all students of naval warfare have recognized. In any other hands than Nelson's, and against another opponent than Villeneuve, they could have led to disaster, to such an appalling risk did they oppose the leading ships of each line. But the risk was calculated. Nelson had always worked to a low factor of safety. He knew his fleet, and he knew his opponents. He had seized the essence – 'laying his ships well on board the enemy as expeditiously as possible' – and that was what he did. There were extraordinary incidents in the process, tensions, comedy, pride, tragedy, triumph, and it is fortunate that so many were recorded.

The *Victory*'s surgeon, William Beatty, wrote that 'soon after daylight, Lord Nelson came upon deck. He was dressed as usual in his Admiral's frockcoat, bearing on the left breast four stars of different Orders, which he always wore with his common apparel. He did not wear his sword in the Battle of Trafalgar. It had been taken from the place where it hung up in his cabin, and was laid ready on his table; but it is supposed he forgot to call for it. This was the only action in which he ever appeared without a sword. He displayed excellent spirits, and expressed his pleasure at the prospect of giving a fatal blow to the naval power of France and Spain; and spoke with confidence of obtaining a signal victory notwithstanding the inferiority of the British fleet, declaring to Captain Hardy that "he would not be contented with capturing less than twenty sail of the line". He afterwards pleasantly observed that "the 21st of October was the happiest day in the year among his family" but did not assign the reason for this. His lordship had previously entertained a strong presentiment that this would prove the auspicious day, and had several times said to Captain Hardy and Dr Scott (chaplain of the Ship and Foreign Secretary to the Commander-in-Chief, whose intimate friendship he enjoyed) "the 21st of October will be our day!" '

The family occasion of which Nelson was thinking was an action which had taken place in West Indian waters in 1757, during the Seven Years War. His maternal uncle, Captain Suckling, under whom he had himself first gone to sea, made his name in command of the *Dreadnought*, when three British ships had attacked seven French vessels, and severely damaged them. Nelson also told his retinue that it pleased him to think that this was the day of the annual fair at Burnham Thorpe, his Norfolk birthplace.

When Blackwood arrived, he 'had the satisfaction to find the Admiral in good but very calm spirits. After receiving my congratulations at the approach of the moment he so often and so long had wished for, he replied: "I mean today to bleed the captains of the Frigates, as I shall keep you on board until the very last minute." His mind seemed entirely directed to the strength and formation of the Enemy's line, as well as to the effects which his novel mode of attack was likely to produce.'

Owing to disadvantage of light, Villeneuve had been about ten minutes later than Nelson in gaining a clear view of the fleet to which he was opposed. When he did so, it appeared to be in no recognizable formation. Then it divided, in accordance with Nelson's signal, steering for his centre and rear. Villeneuve now had to face the fact that if he held his immediate course he would be committed to the passage of the Straits, with Nelson hard in pursuit, and with the likelihood of further ships from Gibraltar disputing his intention. He took the action which Nelson had expected. Although his fleet was still in some disorder, Villeneuve reversed its course, heading it northwards, towards Cadiz. But already he was too late. The movement took too long; and Commodore Churruca, commanding the *San Juan de Nepomuceno*, now the rear ship of the Allied line, turned to his second in command with the words: 'The fleet is doomed. The French admiral does not understand his business. He has compromised us all.' He was not alone in his opinion. But placed as he was, and with Nelson set on battle, Villeneuve's problem had no satisfactory solution unless, by some miracle, the wind dropped, and night at length masked his retreat.

Nelson had every reason to be cheerful. His problems

seemed over. He had gained the wish of his heart, the opportunity to defeat a principal fleet in the open sea. 'At daylight,' ran the famous last entry in his private diary, 'saw the Enemy's Combined Fleet from east to ESE; bore away; made the signal for Order of Sailing and to Prepare for Battle. The Enemy with their heads to the southward. At seven the Enemy wearing in succession. May the Great God whom I worship, grant to my Country, and for the benefit of Europe in general, a great and glorious Victory; and may no misconduct in anyone tarnish it; and may humanity after Victory be the predominant feature in the British Fleet. For myself individually, I commit my life to Him who made me, and may His blessing light upon my endeavours for serving my Country faithfully. To Him I resign myself, and the just cause which is entrusted me to defend. Amen, Amen, Amen.'

I I

Having composed his prayer, and added a codicil to his will which stated his view of Lady Hamilton's services to her country, a document which was witnessed by Black-wood and Hardy, Nelson had leisure to see and approve Hardy's arrangements for fighting the *Victory*. He visited every deck, spoke to the men at quarters, exchanged greet-ings with special friends, and made everyone cheerful and confident.

As the morning drew on, there were continual signals, first from Collingwood and later from Nelson, for ships to make more sail. The flagships were leading their respective lines, though this was not in accordance with the Memo-randum, and it was a fact which added a touch of comedy to the proceedings. Blackwood at one time had urged Nel-son to transfer his flag to a frigate, and when the idea was rejected by the admiral on the score of example, he was persuaded to argue that the *Téméraire* should precede the

Victory into action. Yet Nelson would permit no taking in of sail, such as would have allowed the ships to change places, and when, at the last moment, Captain Harvey was on the point of overtaking, Nelson actually signalled him astern by flag, one account says by hailing in person as well.

Earlier in the day he had seen that Collingwood, in the *Royal Sovereign*, was beginning to outstrip the ships of his line by a considerable margin, and he grew so anxious for his old friend that he signalled to Duff of the *Mars*, which was fast, to draw ahead of his admiral. The order was without effect, for Collingwood, like Nelson, refused to take in sail. Nelson himself had packed his punch. There were three three-decked ships at the head of his line, the *Victory*, the *Téméraire* and the *Neptune*; Collingwood had no such powerful close support, for his other three-deckers, the *Dreadnought* and the *Prince*, were nowhere near the van of his squadron.

At 11.40 Nelson telegraphed to Collingwood announcing: 'I intend to pass through the enemy's line to prevent them getting into Cadiz,' an action in which he was to be foiled by the close formation of the Allies. This was followed by a general signal to: 'Make all sail with safety to the masts.' It was clear that some ships were intent on keeping the arranged 'Order of Battle'. Nelson's view was that even a moment's delay in grappling with an opponent might mean the loss of a prize. John Pasco, who was acting as signal lieutenant, was having a busy morning. He had already been concerned in one incident which affected his own future; he was soon to be involved in another, which has become legendary.

Pasco could have been doing duty as first lieutenant of the *Victory*, to which seniority entitled him, but in order to avoid a succession of executive officers, he had agreed to waive his rank while serving on Nelson's staff. The position was acceptable, at any rate as a temporary measure, in the course of a routine commission, but when a general action was in prospect it was a different matter, for the senior lieutenant would be sure to gain promotion if he survived, possibly to post-captain.

During the morning, Pasco had to make a report to Lord Nelson. 'On entering the Cabin,' so he afterwards told Sir Harris Nicolas, 'I discovered his lordship on his knees, writing. He was then penning that beautiful prayer. I waited until he rose, and communicated what I had to report, but could not, at such a moment, disturb his mind with any grievance of mine.' Pasco's delicacy cost him years of seniority in captain's rank, for he was only made a commander after the battle, Quilliam, the first lieutenant, receiving a double step, while poor Pasco had to wait for this. But he lived to become an admiral, and on the day of Trafalgar he ordered the hoist of Nelson's best-known message.

Blackwood records that as he was walking with Nelson on the poop the admiral said: 'I'll now amuse the Fleet with a signal,' asking his friend if he did not think there was one yet wanting. Blackwood said he thought that everyone seemed clearly to understand what they were about, but Nelson kept to his opinion. 'His lordship came to me on the poop,' Pasco afterwards related, 'and about a quarter to noon said: "I wish to say to the Fleet, ENGLAND CONFIDES THAT EVERY MAN WILL DO HIS DUTY"; and he added: "You must be quick, for I have one more to make, which is for Close Action." I replied, "If your lordship will permit me to substitute *expects* for *confides*, the signal will soon be completed, because the word 'expects' is in the vocabulary, and 'confides' must be spelt." His lordship replied, in haste, and with seeming satisfaction: "That will do, Pasco, make it directly!" When it had been answered by a few ships in the Van, he ordered me to make the signal for Close Action, and to *keep it up*: accordingly, I hoisted No. 16 at the top-gallant mast-head, and there it

remained until shot away.' There was, in fact, one inter-
mediate signal made. This was to 'Prepare to anchor at
close of day.' Nelson knew the danger of a lee shore, in this
case the Shoals of Trafalgar, especially to battle-damaged
ships, and he believed that by nightfall there might be a
gale of wind.

The effect of the famous hoist was various. According to
one account, Nelson was delighted with his own inspiration. 'Now,' he said, 'I can do no more. We must trust to
the great Disposer of all events, and the justice of our
cause! I thank God for this great opportunity of doing my
duty!' But in the *Victory*, below decks, when the words
were repeated by an officer of marines, some of the men –
though they cheered – were nonplussed. Had they not
always done their duty? Were they likely to falter now? As
for Collingwood, his biographer reports that when the
admiral saw it first, he said that he wished Nelson would
make no more signals, for they all understood what they
were to do! But in the Journal of Captain Redmill of the
Polyphemus he noted that when the message was given to
the ship's company it 'was answered with three cheers, and
answered by the *Dreadnought* on our starboard beam,' and
when Napoleon heard that Nelson had flown it in battle, he
ordered a similar message to be painted in a prominent
place on all his own ships.

Soon after this incident the frigate captains took their
leave. Blackwood was ordered to tell 'all the captains of
Line-of-Battle Ships that Nelson depended on their exertions; and that if, by the mode of attack prescribed, they
found it impracticable to get into Action immediately, they
might adopt whatever they thought best, provided it led
them quickly and closely alongside an Enemy. He then
again desired me to go away; and as we were standing on
the front of the poop, I took his hand, and said, "I trust,
my Lord, that on my return to the *Victory*, which will be
as soon as possible, I shall find your Lordship well, and in

possession of twenty Prizes." On which he made this reply: "God bless you, Blackwood, I shall never speak to you again." '

Within a few minutes, the *Royal Sovereign* came under concentrated fire. '*Here began the Din of War....*' The words are from the journal of Lieutenant Barclay of the *Britannia*. That Din did not cease until darkness, and until the day was decided by gunnery at short range, by boarding, or by a combination of the two.

III

In the *Royal Sovereign* Collingwood's hours had been less dramatic, at least until the time of encounter, than that of the Commander-in-Chief in the *Victory*, but equally characteristic. Mr Smith, the admiral's servant, entered the cabin about daybreak and found his master 'already up and dressing'. Collingwood asked Smith if he had seen the French fleet. 'On my replying that I had not,' so Smith recorded, 'he told me to look out at them, adding that in a very short time we should see a great deal more.... I then observed a crowd of ships to leeward; but I could not help looking with still greater interest at the Admiral, who during all this time was shaving himself with a composure which quite astonished me....'

Collingwood dressed himself that morning with particular care, and soon afterwards, meeting Lieutenant Clavell, who was a favourite with him, advised him to pull off his boots. 'You had better put on silk stockings, as I have done,' he said, 'for if one should get a shot in the leg, they would be so much more manageable for the surgeon.' He then proceeded to visit the decks, and addressing the officers said to them in his sober way: 'Now, gentlemen, let us do something today which the world may talk of hereafter.'

It was Collingwood's belief that if a ship could fire three

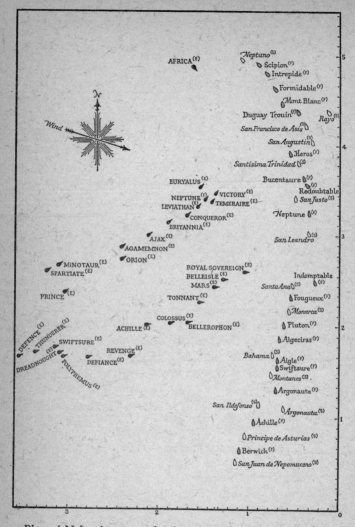

Plan of Nelson's approach: the position of the two fleets at noon on October 21st, 1805, showing the ships of the line and the 'Euryalus' frigate

well-directed broadsides in five minutes, no enemy could resist them, and in the *Dreadnought* he had been able to cut down the time to three minutes and a half. The *Royal Sovereign*, fresh from home, could not yet equal that speed, but her gunnery was already creditable, and was to show itself remarkable in battle. When, from his windward station, Nelson saw his friend beginning to come under close fire, he exclaimed: 'See how that noble fellow, Collingwood, takes his ship into action. How I envy him!'

Hercules Robinson, then a midshipman in the *Euryalus*, came to know Collingwood well, and was fond of telling how in action he walked the break of the poop 'with his little triangular gold-laced cocked hat, tights, silk stockings and buckles, musing over the progress of the fight, and munching an apple'. As Robinson said, an admiral's principal business took place before and after an engagement. During its course, the burden was on the individual captains.

Collingwood's instructions had been to pass through the enemy line at the twelfth ship from the rear, but seeing that the ship in question was a two-decker, and that the next ahead was the great *Santa Ana*, which carried the flag of Admiral Alava, he chose her as his point of attack. The *Fougueux*, immediately astern, closed up, and when Collingwood saw the movement he ordered Rotheram, the captain of the *Royal Sovereign*, to steer straight at the Frenchman and carry away his bowsprit. To avoid this, the *Fougueux* backed her main top-sail, and allowed Collingwood to pass through, at the same time beginning her own fire. Collingwood ordered a gun to be fired occasionally at her, in order to cover his own ship with smoke. Then, ranging alongside the Spaniard, he gave her a broadside and a half, killing and wounding about a hundred men, and in a matter of seconds the lower yards of the two ships were locked together. At one point, a top-gallant studding-sail, which had been shot away, was hanging over the gangway hammocks. Collingwood called out to Clavell to come and help him take it in, observing that they should want it some other day! The two officers rolled it carefully up, and placed it in a boat. By half-past two, after a fight which had lasted more than two hours, much of it at the closest quarters, the *Santa Ana* struck. By that time the *Royal Sovereign* was herself so damaged that she called on the *Euryalus*, whose captain had a way of being at the critical point, to take her in tow, and to make any necessary signals. Just before nightfall, when Collingwood had heard from Hardy's own lips of Nelson's fate, he transferred in person to the frigate, where he remained until the *Queen*, a three-decker, was available for his flag.

Collingwood said of the *Santa Ana* that she was a 'Spanish perfection. . . . She towered over the *Royal Sovereign* like a castle. No ship fired a shot at her but ourselves, and you have no conception how completely she was ruined.' Careful of his own property, as of that of the Admiralty, Collingwood had a serio-comic tale of destruction to tell a friend after the battle. 'I have had a great destruction of my furniture and stock,' he said. 'I have hardly a chair that has not a shot in it, and many have lost both legs and arms, without hope of pension. My wine broke in moving, and my pigs were slain in battle; and these are heavy losses where they cannot be replaced.'

The admiral perhaps claimed too much when he said that the *Royal Sovereign* alone engaged the *Santa Ana*, for the *Belleisle*, which followed Collingwood's lead as closely as she could, fired her first port broadside into Alava's ship, and her starboard into the *Fougueux*, which was now drifting to leeward. The *Belleisle* was on the point of raking another ship, the *Indomptable*, when the *Fougueux* loomed back out of the smoke, and struck her starboard gangway with her port bow, rolling her foreyard over the quarter-deck. The *Indomptable* then crossed the *Belleisle*'s bows, gave her a broadside, and drifted away. When she had gone, the *Belleisle* and *Fougueux* lay locked together for the greater part of an hour.

With the third ship it went hard: she was the *Mars*, and it was the *Fougueux* which did much of the damage. As she dropped to leeward after her encounter with the *Royal Sovereign*, she came into a position where she could rake the *Mars*. The captain of marines, Norman, who was on the poop, went to the quarter-deck to report the situation to Captain Duff, who asked if any of their own guns would bear on the *Fougueux*. Norman said: 'I think not, but I cannot see for smoke.' 'Then,' said Duff, 'we must point our guns at the ships on which they *can* bear. I shall go and look, but the men below may see better, as there is less smoke.' Duff went to the end of the quarter-deck to peer over the side, and then ordered a messenger to go below and tell the gunners to train more aft. 'He had scarcely turned round,' wrote an eye-witness, 'when the *Fougueux* raked the *Mars*. A cannon shot killed Duff, and two seamen who were immediately behind him. The ball struck the captain on the chest, and carried off his head. His body fell on the gangway, where it was covered with a spare colour until after the action.' As Lieutenant Duff was also killed in the battle, poor young Norwich was the only member of his family left alive in the ship. A little later Captain Cosmao of the *Pluton* gave the *Mars* another broadside, which completed the destruction of her masts and rigging. She drifted away, unmanageable. Grim sentences in her log tell her story more graphically than any formal account. 'At 1.15 Captain Duff was killed and the poop and Quarter Deck almost left destitute the Carnage was so great having every One of our Braces and Running Rigging shot away which made the Ship entirely ungovernable and was frequently raked by different Ships of the Enemy.' It was well that Captain Duff, as one of his last actions, had ordered his son below.

Successive ships followed the example of the *Royal Sovereign*, the *Belleisle* and the *Mars*, until the whole of the Allied rear was closely engaged, or had been driven to leeward. Seldom had there been a series of such grim encounters.

It was characteristic of sea fighting in the days of sail that gunfire itself hardly ever sank a ship, and that broadsides rarely damaged the wooden hulls of ships of the line beyond repair. They struck their colours to an opponent more often because they were raked, that is, riddled from end to end by fire from astern or ahead, a process which dismounted guns and caused immense casualties along the decks, or because they were boarded and taken hand-to-hand, or because their masts and rigging were shot away, so that they became a prey to the natural hazards of the sea, unless their battle-weary and depleted crews could improvise jury-rigs, or anchor in security, or call upon a friendly tow. Battles under sail were clumsy, stubborn, protracted and grim beyond belief.

Collingwood had given an example of how a flagship should be fought, and his line, in spite of the hammering suffered by the leading ships, succeeded in its allotted task. What of Nelson, whose business it was to prevent interruption of the work of his second in command? He had old his friend Lord Sidmouth: 'Rodney broke the line in one point. I will break it in two.'

IV

Major-General Théodore Contamine, the senior military officer who sailed with Villeneuve, wrote an account some weeks after the action, for the benefit of the French Ministry of Marine. This is inaccurate in many details, but the general, as a soldier, had the advantage of being able to write objectively, while as a prisoner of war he had had opportunities of talking over the battle with his captors.

His story of Nelson's approach differed in several respects from that of others.

'Admiral Nelson,' he wrote, 'had been begged by the officers of his fleet to form his two columns with greater regularity; they were bearing down without formation on our line; but he, as became a genius, felt too keenly how essential it was to take prompt advantage of any favourable opportunity that presented itself.' Contamine maintained that, before the action became general, the wind was so light that it was almost impossible for the Combined Fleet to keep any steerage-way, when standing close-hauled to the wind: '... the enemy fleet, on the contrary, with a stern wind and carrying a press of sail, were able to profit by what little air was stirring and by the swell to bear down on us, to take up such positions as they chose, to direct their principal attacks against one point or another of our line, to disable some of our ships to commence with, to overwhelm them in detail, and to defeat them thus one after another.'

Contamine continued: 'So many advantages, which a little breeze would have unexpectedly dissipated, could not fail to be seized upon by Nelson, and could he tarry one minute in profiting by them, solely for the purpose of getting into more regular order? The results unhappily justify only too well the decision he had taken to attack without delay.'

The French view of Nelson was that he was impetuous. Villeneuve had before him an official appreciation of the admiral's character which gave Nelson little credit for brains, though some for trusting his officers, and much for bravery. 'The enemy will not trouble to form line parallel to ours and fight it out with the gun,' Villeneuve himself had written, with memories of the Nile in mind. 'He will try to double our rear, cut through the line, and bring against the ships thus isolated, groups of his own to surround and capture them. Captains must rely on their courage and love of glory, rather than upon the signals of the Admiral, who may already be engaged and wrapped in smoke. . . . The captain who is not in action is not at his post.' Conditions at the Nile and at Trafalgar were widely different, but Villeneuve was right in his idea that, whatever the circumstances, Nelson would never tolerate a battle on the old formal pattern. Almost any risk was preferable to that.

Knowledge of this fact, on Villeneuve's part, presented him with the unwelcome certainty that, if once a 'pell-mell' action was joined, no planned tactics, however skilled, could save his fleet. All would depend on individual capacity for fighting, and that was where Nelson, with his incomparable experience, believed that he had an overwhelming advantage.

Once committed to his attack, and having given his order to anchor after action or at nightfall, Nelson had nothing but details to attend to as he waited for the punishment which would be the inevitable result of his head-on approach to the enemy. He had already seen Collingwood face it, and for all he knew, Collingwood himself might already have been slain.

Nelson, tense by now, showed acute interest in detail, as he did so often under stress, never hesitating to interfere directly with the running of the ship in a way which might have exasperated a less phlegmatic flag-captain than Hardy. He rated a lieutenant for what he thought was taking in a studding-sail, though in point of fact it was being set afresh. Shortly before the opening shots were fired at the *Victory*, so one of the midshipmen recorded, Nelson ordered that the hammocks which were stowed along the side should be thoroughly soused with water, a wise measure against fire. During the process, one of the seamen, too free with his bucket, splashed the uniform of an officer of marines who was stationed on the poop, and got cursed for his carelessness. Nelson overheard, and took the seaman's part, telling the marine officer that it was his own fault for getting in the way, and that he wished he had had the whole lot! Within a few minutes, at about 12.15, the *Victory* came under fire from the *Heros*, and the hammocks were soon proving their use against fragments of shot.

Shortly before Blackwood returned to his frigate Nelson asked him, as he had done several times before, what he would consider a victory satisfactory in the circumstances. He never, he said, doubted the outcome for an instant, despite the bold way the enemy were standing up to him, though he questioned the possibility of being able to save many prizes. Blackwood answered that 'considering the handsome way in which battle was offered by the Enemy, and their apparent determination for a fair trial of strength, with the proximity of the land, I thought if fourteen ships were captured it would be a glorious result'. Nelson replied: 'I shall not, Blackwood, be satisfied with anything short of twenty.'

Soon the Union flags, and the white ensigns which had been flown in general actions since St Vincent's victory of February 14th, 1797, were seen on every ship,* and at 12.24 the *Victory*, nearly fifteen minutes after she had herself come under fire, opened with her starboard guns.

Throughout the near approach, every eye aboard the *Victory* had been looking for the ship wearing the flag of the Allied commander-in-chief – and apparently in vain. But at Trafalgar, everything seemed destined to befit a final battle conducted by Nelson, and he broke upon the French line – though not, as he had planned, through it –

---

* Nelson, as a vice-admiral of the White, would have flown a white ensign in the *Victory* in the ordinary way, though Collingwood, as a vice-admiral of the Blue, would have flown a blue flag. The explanation of the practice, since 1797, of ships flying white ensigns in action was so that there should be no confusion with the flags of Spain or France, which could be mistaken at a distance for red and blue ensigns respectively.

close to the *Bucentaure*. But before that event, much had happened.

Bands had struck up with stirring tunes, 'Rule Britannia', 'Britons Strike Home', 'Heart of Oak'. The gunners had stripped to the waist and tied handkerchiefs round their heads to deaden the noise of their pieces; others sharpened cutlasses; others even danced the hornpipe. Veterans, peering through the ports, recognized in the distance old acquaintances such as the *Santissima Trinidad*, dazzling in vermilion and white, and thought what fine prizes they would look at Spithead. Hardy had asked Nelson, probably at Dr Beatty's suggestion, whether he did not think that the four stars of chivalry on his admiral's coat did not make him too conspicuous, and Nelson had answered that no doubt it was true, but that it was no time to be changing it.

Ranging shots from the enemy at first fell short, then alongside, then over. Soon they began to hit, though, in the accepted style of the French, the aim was high. It was masts and sails they wished to damage, since this affected an opponent's speed. One of the early casualties was John Scott, Nelson's Public Secretary, who was cut almost in two by a round shot, as he spoke with Hardy on the quarter deck. His body was thrown overboard, though not before Nelson had exclaimed: 'Is that poor Scott!' Whipple, the captain's clerk, was shortly afterwards killed by blast, and the marines on the poop began to suffer badly until, by Nelson's order, they were moved to positions less exposed. Soon the *Victory*'s sails were riddled, and her wheel smashed. Throughout the rest of the action the ship was steered from the gun-room, by tiller, an emergency which called for the services of many hands. 'This is too warm work, Hardy, to last long,' said Nelson with a smile, and he congratulated his captain on the fact that, in all the battles he had been in, he had never seen more cool courage than was being shown by the company around him.

The *Victory*'s counter-stroke, though inevitably delayed, was fierce. About twenty minutes after she first opened fire, she passed across the stern of the *Bucentaure*. She fired her forecastle carronade into the cabin windows, and followed up with a double-shotted broadside. The smoke blew back in a choking cloud. Dust from broken woodwork covered the quarter-deck, and gun-crews listened with professional satisfaction to the crash of shot from end to end of the French flagship. The *Santa Ana* had not fared worse at Collingwood's hands, and the effect of the concentrated fire left the *Bucentaure* an easy prey to other ships.

Near Villeneuve's flagship was the French *Neptune*, which raked the *Victory*'s bows as she came round to starboard and ran on board the *Redoutable*, which had also kept station close to her admiral. Nelson had said to Hardy: 'It does not signify which we run on board of. Take your choice!' The *Redoutable*'s captain, seeing that the *Victory*'s lower guns were active, while her upper ones were almost silent from loss among the crews, shut most of her lower gun ports, but kept her main deck guns firing, and rained shot from her fighting-tops. Soon the two ships were firmly held together by an entanglement in their rigging, and both crews were anxious to board, but the French were prevented by the *Victory*'s starboard carronade, and by a broadside from the *Téméraire*, and the English by musketry and grenades, which made the upper deck almost untenable.

The *Victory* had already disabled the vessel she would have chosen, of all others, to encounter. She was now at grips with the best trained ship in the entire Allied line, commanded by Captain Jean Lucas.

V

The battle had begun to resolve into its differing phases. Collingwood, with fifteen ships, engaged the enemy rear.

Nelson, with twelve, contained the van, of which the leading ships under Dumanoir stood at first so far to the
northward that they could take no part in the action. They
were later turned, with much difficulty in the light air, and
bore down with the intention of a counter-attack, a threat
which was beaten off. The remainder of the day was given
to the taking and manning of prizes, and to rendering
serviceable such English ships as had been badly mauled.
Never was a pell-mell battle better named, or better justified. No English ship hauled down her colours, but there
was a time when, at the very centre of the struggle, there
came acute crisis and tragedy. The credit of bringing this
about belonged mainly to one ship, and it is seemly that
her story should be distinguished from that of others.

VI

The record of the French *Redoutable* at Trafalgar is one of
the finest in the history of any navy. She fought two three-
deckers, immobilized one of them, the *Victory*, and fired
the shot which killed Nelson. For a 74-gun ship, the feat
was brilliant almost beyond belief.

Before he made his way out of Cadiz, Villeneuve, listing
his fleet, said of the *Redoutable* that she was 'a fine ship, fit
for any employment'. The words were exact. Her narrative
is best told in the report of her captain, Lucas, who survived the battle many years.

'Ever since the *Redoutable* was fitted out,' so he wrote
from England, 'no measures had been neglected to train the
crew in every sort of drill. My ideas were always directed
towards fighting by boarding. I so counted upon its success
that everything had been prepared to undertake it with advantage. I had had canvas pouches to hold two grenades
made for all captains of guns; the cross-belts of these
pouches carried a tin tube containing a small match. In all
our drills, I made them throw a great number of paste-

board grenades, and I often landed the grenadiers in order to have them explode iron grenades. They had so acquired the habit of hurling them that on the day of battle our topmen were throwing two at a time.

'I had 100 carbines fitted with long bayonets on board. The men to whom these were served out were so well accustomed to their use that they climbed half-way up the shrouds to open musketry fire. All those armed with swords were given broadsword practice every day, and pistols became familiar weapons to them. The grapnels were thrown so skilfully that they would succeed in hooking a ship even though not exactly touching us. When the drum beat to quarters, each man went to his station fully armed, and with his weapons loaded; he placed them near his gun in nettings nailed between each beam. Finally the crew had themselves such confidence in this manner of fighting that they often urged me to board the first ship with which we should engage.'

Even before the battle Lucas had had the chance to show his alertness. On October 20th, when the *Redoutable* was some distance in the wake of the *Bucentaure*, the flagship signalled: 'Man overboard.' 'I immediately hove-to,' said Lucas, 'and lowered a boat, which saved the man who had fallen into the sea. I signalled the same at once, and a little later I resumed my station.'

Once in action, Lucas 'laid the *Redoutable*'s bowsprit against the *Bucentaure*'s stern, fully resolved to sacrifice my ship in defence of the admiral's flag. I acquainted my officers and crew, who replied to my decision by shouts of '*Vive L'Empereur! Vive l'Amiral! Vive le Commandant!*' repeated a thousand times. Preceded by the drums and fifes that I had on board, I paraded at the head of my executive round the deck; everywhere I found gallant lads burning with impatience to begin the fray, many of them saying: "Captain, don't forget to board!"'

Lucas could not prevent the *Victory* from raking the

Bucentaure, but when she ran aboard the *Redoutable*, the two ships closed so that the Frenchman's poop was abeam of the *Victory*'s quarter-deck. 'In this position,' said Lucas, 'the grapnels were flung. Those aft were cut loose, but those forward held. Our broadsides were fired muzzle to muzzle, and there resulted a horrible carnage.' Soon Lucas 'ordered the trumpet to sound. It was the recognized signal to summon the boarding parties in our exercises. They came up in such perfect order, with the officers and mid-shipmen at the head of their divisions, that one would have said it was only a sham fight. In less than a minute the upper works were covered with armed men who hurled themselves on to the poop, on to the nettings, and into the shrouds.' For some moments the *Victory* was in danger, but the ships were rolling, and her height made it difficult for the eager French to cross. 'I gave orders to cut away the slings of the main yard and to lower it to serve as a bridge,' said Lucas. 'Mr Yon, midshipman, and four seamen succeeded in getting on board the *Victory* by means of her anchor.' Captain Adair, of the *Victory*'s marines, then brought up a party from below, and although he himself was killed in leading the repulse, the alarm was soon over. A broadside from the *Téméraire* poured into the *Redoutable*, and she ceased to be a fighting ship, though her resistance was not quite at an end.

'It would be difficult to describe the horrible carnage caused by the murderous broadside,' said Lucas. 'More than 200 of our brave lads were killed or wounded. I was wounded at the same instant, but not so seriously as to prevent me from remaining at my post. . . . A little later a third ship came up and stationed herself astern of the *Redoutable* and fired into us at pistol range; in less than half an hour our ship was so riddled that she seemed to be no more than a mass of wreckage. In this state the *Téméraire* hailed us to strike, and not prolong a useless resistance. I ordered several soldiers who were near me to answer this

'Lord Nelson from Life'

Lord Barham

Captain Fremantle

'Commencement of the Battle of Trafalgar'

The *Victory* to leeward of the *Santissima Trinidad*

'Battle of Trafalgar: Rear Division'

HMS *Victory*: the Lower Gun Deck

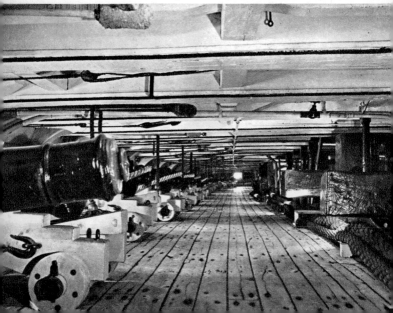

Sir Thomas Hardy

Collingwood

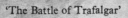
'The Battle of Trafalgar'

Redoutable fighting *Victory* and *Téméraire*

Bucentaure and *Redoutable* firing on *Victory*

Lucas

Magon

The *Belleisle* after the Action

'Victory of Trafalgar: in the Van'

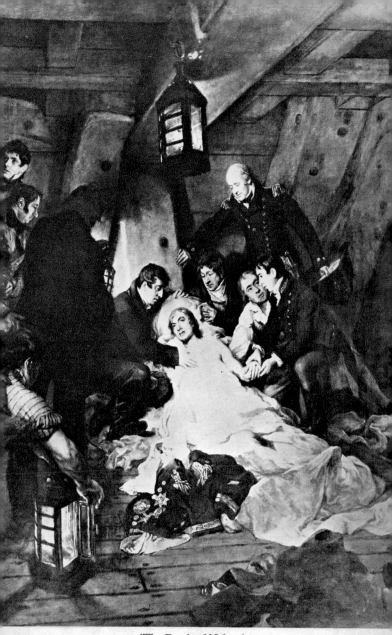

'The Death of Nelson'

Obverse and Reverse of a
Trafalgar Medal by Webb

Nelson's Funeral:
'The Trophied Bier'

summons with musket-shots, which was performed with the greatest zeal. At the very same minute the mainmast fell athwart the *Téméraire*, and that vessel's two topmasts fell on board the *Redoutable*. All the stern was absolutely stove-in, the rudder-stock, the tiller, the two tiller-sweeps, the stern-post, the wing transoms, the transom knees were in general shot to pieces.'

Lucas's description continued: 'All the guns were shattered or dismounted by the shots, or from ships having run us aboard. An 18-pounder gun on the main-deck and a 36-pounder carronade on the forecastle having burst, killed and wounded many of our people. The two sides of the ship, all the lids and bars of the ports were utterly cut to pieces. Four of our six pumps were shattered, as well as our ladders in general, in such sort that communication between the decks and the upper works was extremely difficult. All our decks were covered with dead, buried beneath the debris and the splinters from the different parts of the ship. Out of the ship's company of 643 men we had 522 disabled, 300 being killed and 222 wounded, among whom were almost the entire executive. . . . He who has not seen the *Redoutable* in this state can never have any conception of her destruction.'

'I do not know of anything on board which was not cut up by shot,' Lucas continued. 'In the midst of this carnage the brave lads who had not yet succumbed, and those who were wounded, with whom the orlop-deck was thronged, still cried, *'Vive l'Empereur!* We're not taken yet. Is our Captain still alive?'

Lucas did not strike until he was certain that the leaks were such that his vessel would in any case soon founder. 'At the instant that I was assured of this I ordered the colours to be hauled down. They came down of themselves, with the fall of the mizzen mast.' The *Redoutable, Victory* and *Téméraire* were by then still locked together; they had been joined by the *Fougueux*, which was quite out of control.

So ended the fiercest scene of the entire battle. Lucas's account of his casualties differed from the official return (490 killed: 81 wounded), but she had the highest in the Combined Fleet. Her men died in trying to prevent Nelson from carrying out his intention of passing through the enemy line, and cutting them off from Cadiz. One of them put an end to his life.

At about 1.15, which was nearly half an hour after the *Victory* had become embroiled with the Frenchman, Nelson and Hardy were still steadily pacing the quarter-deck. Already a shot, striking the fore-brace bits, had passed between them, and a splinter had bruised Hardy's foot, tearing off the buckle from his shoe. Just as the pair had arrived within a pace or so of their regular turning point at the cabin ladder-way, Nelson, who regardless of the usual custom was walking on the port side, suddenly faced about.

Hardy, as soon as he had taken one more step, turned, and saw his friend in the act of falling. He was on his knees, with his left hand just touching the deck. Then his arm gave way, and he fell on his left side, exactly at the spot where Scott had been killed earlier in the battle. 'They have done for me at last, Hardy,' said Nelson. 'My backbone is shot through.' The wound was from a musket ball which had entered the left shoulder through the forepart of the epaulette, and, penetrating, had lodged in the spine. The piece had been fired from the *Redoutable*'s mizzen top, the marksman being about fifteen yards away. Serjeant Secker of the marines, together with some seamen, at once bore Nelson down to the cockpit.

Even as he was carried below, Nelson's thoughtfulness for detail did not desert him. First he covered over his face with a handkerchief, so that the men should not be discouraged at the sight of the commander-in-chief laid low. Then, on his way down, he noticed from beneath the covering that the tiller-ropes needed to be re-rove, and asked a midshipman to tell Hardy to see to it. In the *Victory*, most of the damage and almost all the casualties had been confined to the upper deck. Below, the gunners were still ready and able to take on all comers, and they were firing occasionally on the side not in contact with the *Redoutable*.

VII

In order of going into action the British squadrons had formed as follows: Collingwood, leading in the *Royal Sovereign*, was supported by the *Belleisle, Mars, Tonnant, Bellerophon, Colossus, Achille, Revenge, Defiance, Polyphemus, Dreadnaught, Swiftsure, Thunderer* and *Defence*. The *Prince* counted as among the ships destined to attack the rear of the enemy, but in fact her course appears to have lain somewhere between that of Collingwood and that of Nelson, and she came into action so late that by the time she did so, all order had long since crumbled.

Nelson, leading in the *Victory*, was supported by the *Téméraire, Neptune, Leviathan, Conqueror, Britannia, Ajax, Agamemnon, Orion, Minotaur* and *Spartiate*. His remaining ship, the little *Africa*, had lost touch with the main body of the fleet during the night of October 20th. She was on her own, well to the northward of Nelson, who signalled to her, after action had been joined, to 'Make all sail possible with safety to the masts'. Her part in the battle was in fact out of all proportion to her size.

The Combined Fleet were attacked as they ranged in the following order: *Neptuno* (Spanish), *Scipion* (French), *Intrépide* (French), *Formidable* (French), *Mont Blanc* (French), *Duguay Trouin* (French), *Rayo* (Spanish), *San Francisco de Asis* (Spanish), *San Augustin* (Spanish), *Heros* (French), *Santissima Trinidad* (Spanish), *Bucentaure* (French), *Redoutable* (French), *San Justo* (Spanish), *Neptune* (French), *San Leandro* (Spanish), *Santa Ana*

(Spanish), *Indomptable* (French), *Fougueux* (French), *Monarca* (Spanish), *Pluton* (French), *Algéciras* (French), *Bahama* (Spanish), *Aigle* (French), *Swiftsure* (French), *Montanez* (Spanish), *Argonaute* (French), *San Ildefonso* (Spanish), *Argonauta* (Spanish), *Achille* (French), *Principe de Asturias* (Spanish), *Berwick* (French), and *San Juan de Nepomuceno* (Spanish).

It is not to be wondered at that the nomenclature among the ships has led to some confusion. For instance, there was a French *Argonaute* and a Spanish *Argonauta*. The *Algéciras*, which might have been thought to be Spanish, was in fact French. There was a French *Swiftsure* and *Achille*, and British ships of the same name. There was a French *Neptune*, a Spanish *Neptuno* and an English *Neptune*; and while the *Berwick* was French, the *Tonnant*, *Téméraire* and *Spartiate* were in Nelson's fleet.

According to her own account – and the time-keeping in the fleets was anything but synchronized – the *Africa*, detached as she was, came into action not long after the *Royal Sovereign*. 'Engaged the headmost Ship of the Enemies Van,' wrote Captain Henry Digby in his Journal, 'a Spanish two Decker bearing the Flag of an Admiral' (she was actually the *Neptuno*, Commodore Valdez), 'and engaged the whole of the Enemies Van line as we passed them.' Just before she opened fire, the *Africa* 'hove overboard one hundred and three Bags bread two Casks Beef 3 Casks of Pork one Cask of Oatmeal One Cask Suet One Cask Sugar Ten Butts Seven Puncheons twelve hogsheads Ten Lemon Juice Cases' – so Digby continued in his breathless way. Thus lightened, the *Africa* bore down to 'the Assistance of the *Neptune* engaging the *Santissima Trinidada*'. The *Africa* was now mixed up in a battle of giants, for Captain Fremantle's three-decker, third in Nelson's line, was worthy of her huge antagonist. 'At 1.58,' so Digby noted with satisfaction, 'the whole of her Masts went by the Board. When she struck, sent Lieut Smith with a party to take charge of her: at the same time Observed the Enemies Van hauling on the Starboard Tack.' Digby was wrong; the Spaniard had not yet struck, though it was true enough that Dumanoir was at last coming down to the help of his friends.

Unintentionally the *Africa* had played her part in distracting part of the Allied line, and as she suffered severely, there was some justice in her sending a party to the tall Spaniard. But Admiral Cisneros would have felt it beneath his dignity to surrender to a mere 64, and Lieutenant Smith returned to his ship, having been assured, in polite Castilian, that his visit was premature.

But the *Africa* still had a part to play, for she came into action at the final and most critical stage of the *mêlée*. 'It must be some time,' so Nelson had written in his Memorandum, 'before they – the enemy Van – could perform a manoeuvre to bring their force compact to attack any part of the British fleet.' As usual, he had gauged rightly, but the Van would turn in time, and then the fire of such detached ships as the *Africa* would be invaluable.

It was only by using boats, and towing, that some of Dumanoir's ships could be got round at all, and it was nearly three o'clock before they were standing down to the scene of action. By that time the back of the Allies' resistance had been broken. Yet there was still a chance to redeem the day, for the British ships which had borne the brunt of the engagement were for the most part dismasted hulks, and Nelson himself was lying mortally wounded.

In the extreme rear there seemed the best opportunity for effective interference. Here the action was still hot, and Gravina, in the *Principe de Asturias*, was holding his own, though against a concentration which was increasing. He himself, like Nelson, had been gravely wounded, but Escano, his Chief of Staff, was keeping up the struggle with obstinate courage. The danger to the Spanish admiral was so acute that when Dumanoir led down to windward, ready to seize any chance that opened, only four ships followed him, three Frenchmen and the Spanish *Neptuno*. Nearly all the rest made for Gravina to leeward, but one, the *Intrépide*, went straight into the firing which was now dying round the *Bucentaure*. She was checked by the *Africa*, which wore round her stern, ran up her lee side, and quickly made her presence felt. Then fresh ships, the *Ajax* and *Orion* among them, completed the gallant Captain Infernet's discomfiture, and after more resistance, he struck.

By the time Dumanoir was well set in his course there were only the last two ships of Nelson's division, the *Spartiate* and *Minotaur* not yet in close action, and it was these ships which the French admiral thought he might cut off. They saw the danger, but their concern was principally for the *Victory* and the *Téméraire*, as they lay almost helpless, cumbered with wreckage.

Captain Mansfield was leading, in the *Minotaur*, for the order of sailing had been preserved. But the *Minotaur* was slower than the *Spartiate*, and, seeing that there was not a moment to lose, Sir Francis Laforey, who commanded the faster vessel, asked leave to pass. The two ships held straight on across Dumanoir's bows, raking him at pistol shot, and then heaving-to between him and the group round the *Victory*. There they stood their ground, engaging Dumanoir's ships, and forcing them to keep their wind. It was an instance of initiative in the true spirit of Nelson's Memorandum. Dumanoir, finding how much fire-power was left in the centre of the battle, and finding, to his consternation, that the *Bucentaure* had struck, held on to see what could be done in the rear, where Gravina was in such peril.

Collingwood was ready for him. Seeing Dumanoir's threat, he made a general signal for ships to come to the wind in succession on the larboard tack. The result was that by the time Dumanoir was in a position to attack, he saw half a dozen ships hauling out, to form a new line to windward. To depress his spirits still more, he could now see Gravina's flagship bearing away out of action, flying the signal for the fleet to rally round her. Dumanoir, giving up all as lost, held on to the southward, for the Straits of Gibraltar.

By the time Collingwood had news that Nelson was dying, the day was won. Villeneuve and two of his flag-officers were prisoners in the British fleet, and of the thirty-three of the line which had left Cadiz, only eleven got back that night to safety. Four were with Dumanoir: eighteen were still in the area of battle. Seventeen of these ships were largely or totally dismasted, thirteen were actually in possession of prize crews, and one, the French *Achille*, was in flames.

Just as the burning and destruction of the great *Orient* at the battle of the Nile had, with dreadful splendour, illuminated the night of Nelson's first achievement in independent command, so was the fire in the *Achille* symbolic of his victory at Trafalgar. The Frenchman had been engaged in turn by the *Revenge*, *Defiance*, *Swiftsure* and *Polyphemus*. Her captain and most of her officers had been killed or wounded, and at the last she was commanded by a young *Enseigne de Vaisseau*. Then, at about four o'clock, the mighty *Prince*, lumbering late into action, bore down upon her, and fired two raking broadsides into her stern. These brought down her fore- and main-masts, and set her alight.

The *Achille* burnt for an hour and a half. As soon as they saw that the blaze was out of control, boats from the *Prince* rescued as many of her crew as they could, but nothing could save her. Soon her guns, those that were still shotted, were firing on their own, as the heat set off the charges. At sunset she blew up. The sea closed over her wreckage, and the battle was over.

5

The Fortunes of the Ships

AS COLLINGWOOD'S LINE was first in action, it is appropriate to consider the fortune of his ships before those to windward of them, which were led by Nelson.

By the time the *Royal Sovereign* had engaged the *Fougueux, Santa Ana, Indomptable* and others, and had been taken in tow by the *Euryalus*, it was well after two o'clock. The *Royal Sovereign* herself took little further part in the action, though she was at all times ready to drive off French or Spanish ships which ventured too close.

The next astern, *Belleisle*, broke away from her encounter with the *Fougueux* soon after one, when she was engaged in succession by the *Pluton, Aigle, San Justo, San Leandro* and others. Her next protracted duel was with the French *Neptune*. This lasted for three-quarters of an hour, when the Frenchman was driven off by the *Polyphemus*. Captain Hargood in the *Belleisle* had continued to fight splendidly, but it was half miraculous he could still fight at all, considering what the ship had endured as she went into action behind Collingwood. Nelson himself had watched her with admiration, and an officer of marines left an account of the tense moments before she opened fire. 'At a quarter before eleven,' he wrote, 'seven or eight of the enemy's ships opened their fire upon the *Royal Sovereign* and *Belleisle*; and as we were steering directly for them we could only remain passive, and perseveringly approach the position we were to occupy in this great battle. This was a trying moment. Captain Hargood had taken his station on the fore-part of the quarter-deck on the starboard side, occasionally standing on a carronade slide, whence he issued his orders for the men to lie down at their quarters, and with the utmost coolness directed the steering of the ship.

'The silence on board was almost awful, broken only by the firm voice of the captain, "Steady!" or "Starboard a little!" which was repeated by the master to the quarter-master at the helm, and occasionally by an officer calling to the now impatient men: "Lie down there, you, sir!" As we got nearer and nearer to the enemy the silence was, however, broken frequently by the sadly stirring shrieks of the wounded, for of them, and killed, we had more than fifty before we fired a shot; and our colours were three times shot away and rehoisted during the time.

'Seeing our men were fast falling, the first lieutenant ventured to ask Captain Hargood if he had not better show his broadside to the enemy and fire, if only to cover the ship with smoke. The gallant man's reply was somewhat stern, but emphatic: "No. We are ordered to go through the line, and go through she shall, by God!"

'The state of things had lasted about twenty minutes, and it required the tact of the more experienced officers to keep up the spirits of those around them by observing, "We should soon now begin our work," when – like as on another occasion the welcome order was given, "Up, guards, and at 'em!" – our energies were joyfully called into play by "Stand to your guns".'

On the poop, where there were three marine officers, and some thirty men 'at small arms', the order to lie down was not given. One of the junior subalterns wrote: 'The shot began to pass over us, and gave us intimation of what we should in a few minutes undergo. . . . A shriek soon followed – a cry of agony was produced by the next shot – and the loss of the head of a poor recruit was the effect of the succeeding, and, as we advanced, destruction rapidly increased. A severe contusion of the breast now prostrated our captain, but he soon resumed his station. Those only who had been in a similar situation to the one I am attempting to describe can have a correct idea of such a scene.'

Some of the men were in fact now lying down, though not, apparently, by order. 'I was half disposed to follow the example,' continued the lieutenant, but said he, 'turning round, my much esteemed and gallant senior fixed my attention; the serenity of his countenance and the composure with which he paced the deck, drove more than half my terrors away, and, joining him, I became somewhat infused with his spirit, which cheered me on to act the part that became me. My experience is an instance of how much depends on the example of those in command when exposed to the fire of the enemy, more particularly in the trying situation in which we were placed for nearly thirty minutes, from not having the power to retaliate.'

Whether Hargood was right or not in refraining from firing a few guns to help conceal his ship with smoke, the accounts give a representative picture of the ordeal of the leading ships in both lines, and the discipline needed in order to maintain that regular advance which so impressed the enemy.

The *Belleisle*'s last act in the battle was befitting. She took possession of the *Argonauta*, one of the finest of all the Spanish two-deckers. This was one case among many where ships surrendered not to the opponent which had given them mortal wounds, but to an enemy who could take advantage of extreme condition. In this case, the surrender was to a very battered and glorious ship.

In her duel with the *Neptune* the *Belleisle* had lost such masts and rigging as still remained standing, and she was in fact the only ship on the British side to be totally dismasted, being at one point as near destruction as any ship in either fleet. She was then almost unable to fire a gun, owing to wreckage, but an ensign was nailed to the stump of her mizzen, and she kept a Union flag flying at the top of a handspike. As they passed by, late in the battle, the men of the *Spartiate* gave her a cheer, as well they might. Earlier, the *Swiftsure* had come to her help. 'Though an immovable log,' wrote one of the *Swiftsure* lieutenants, 'she still kept up a smart fire upon the enemy whenever it was possible to bring a gun to bear. This was a scene that truly accorded with the feelings of an Englishman.

'When we came up with her,' the account continued, 'the Ship's company was crowded upon the Poop, Quarters and every other part of the Ship to cheer us, which they did by giving loud Huzzas, which we were not dilatory in returning. Captain Hargood then requested our Captain to engage a ship to windward of him that was firing into the *Belleisle*, as it was impossible to return her fire.' The enemy in question was the *Achille*. The *Swiftsure* gave her the attention necessary. Later the *Belleisle* was taken in tow by the frigate *Naiad*, and again came within hail of the *Swiftsure*, when Captain Hargood thanked Captain Rutherford for his help.

There was a significant pause in the log of the *Mars*, soon after she had lost her captain. She asked for a tow from the *Euryalus*, Captain Blackwood replying that he would do it with pleasure, but that he was going to help the Second in Command, by Collingwood's order. The *Mars* then drifted towards the group of ships near the *Victory*, where she received an unexpected honour. The French Commander-in-Chief, together with officers of his retinue, came on board from the *Bucentaure*, and were received by Lieutenant William Hannah, who had succeeded to the command of the ship. The party were later transferred to the *Neptune*, since the *Mars* was in no state to accommodate them. Villeneuve in due course went to the *Euryalus*, and this gave Blackwood the chance of first-hand acquaintance with all the principal leaders in the battle. Nelson he knew well. For Collingwood he was now repeating signals. Soon he would discover the sort of man that Villeneuve was, and would grow to respect him.

Of the adventures of the *Tonnant*, Captain Tyler, there are various descriptions, among them one by Lieutenant Clements, who said that, 'we went down in no order, but every man to take his bird. They cut us up a good deal, until we got our broadside to bear on a Spanish ship in breaking the line, when we gave her such a thundering broadside that she did not return a gun for some minutes, and a very few afterwards.' She was the *Monarca*.

The *Tonnant* next engaged the French *Algéciras*, Magon's flagship. George Sartorious, a midshipman who rose later to become an Admiral of the Fleet, said of his ship, that, 'she was one of the very few, perhaps one of the four or five that had been constantly exercised at her guns. Had we not been well exercised, I think the Frenchman would have got the advantage of us. We had actually our fire-engine playing on her broadside to put out the fire caused by the flame of our guns.'

One of the lieutenants wrote that the *Algéciras* 'in the most gallant manner, locked her bowsprit in our starboard main shrouds and attempted to board us, with the greater part of her officers and ship's company. She had riflemen in her tops, who did great execution. Our poop was soon cleared, and our gallant captain shot through the left thigh and carried below. During this time we were not idle. We gave it her most gloriously with the starboard and main deckers, and turned the forecastle gun, loaded with grape, on the gentlemen who wished to give us a fraternal hug. The marines kept up a warm destructive fire on the boarders. Only one man made good his footing on our quarterdeck, when he was pinned through the calf of his right leg by one of the crew with his half-pike, while another was going to cut him down, which I prevented, and desired him to be taken to the cockpit.

'At length we had the satisfaction of seeing her three lower masts go by the board, as they had been shot through below the deck, and carrying with them all their sharpshooters, to look sharper in the next world; for as all our boats were shot through we could not save one of them. The crew were then ordered, with the second lieutenant, to board her. They cheered, and in a short time carried her. They found the gallant Admiral Magon killed at the foot of the poop ladder, and the captain dangerously wounded. Out of eight lieutenants, five were killed, with three hundred petty officers and seamen, and about one hundred wounded.' The exaggeration is here considerable. The actual casualty figures for the *Algéciras* were seventy-seven killed and one hundred and forty-two wounded. The *Tonnant* had twenty-six killed and fifty wounded. 'During this time,' added Lieutenant Clements, 'we were hard at it on a Spanish ship when at last down came her colours. I hailed him, and asked him if he had struck, when he said, "Yes".'

The *Algéciras* was soon taken possession of by another ship, but meanwhile the *Monarca* had rehoisted her colours, though she gained nothing from her change of mind, for she was soon engaged by the *Bellerophon*, the 'Billy Ruffian' – as her seamen called her. This was a ship which had already distinguished herself at the Glorious First of June and at the Nile. She got into action at the same time as the *Tonnant*, and was soon engaged on both sides. Her larboard broadside was fired at the *Monarca*, while her forward starboard guns were aimed at the *Aigle*. She was then attacked by the *Montanez*, by the French *Swiftsure* and by the *Bahama*. One of her officers reported that while she was thus beset, the '*Aigle* twice attempted to board us, and hove several grenades into our lower deck, which burst and wounded several of our people most dreadfully.

'She likewise set fire to our fore-chains. Our fire was so hot that we soon drove them from the lower deck, after which our people took the quoins out and elevated their guns, so as to tear her decks and sides to pieces. When she got clear of us she did not return a single shot while we raked her; her starboard side was entirely beaten in, and, as we afterwards learnt, four hundred men were *hors de combat*, so that she was an easy conquest for the *Defiance*, a fresh ship.' Once again, the casualties are a wild estimate, but it is known that the *Aigle* lost about two-thirds of her ship's company.

The *Bellerophon* herself suffered severely, having twenty-seven killed, including her captain, and well over a hundred wounded. Much of this loss was caused by the *Aigle*'s grenades exploding loose powder near the guns. 'One of the grenades,' said the first lieutenant, Cumby, 'in its explosion had blown off the scuttle of the gunner's store-room, setting fire to it and forcing open the door into the magazine passage. The door was so placed that the same blast that blew open the store-room door, *shut* the door of the magazine. Otherwise we must all in both ships inevitably have been blown up together.' The gunner, with a small party, got the fire under control, and Lieutenant Cumby took command after Captain Cooke's death. He wrote to his father that some of the men chalked on their guns 'Victory or Death'.

Although the *Monarca* struck to the *Bellerophon* at about two o'clock, she may well have regretted that the *Aigle* was not her prize instead, for according to the *Bellerophon* the *Aigle* was the best-manned ship in the Combined Fleet, and they thought themselves the same. Certainly the two ships in the British fleet which lost their captains, the *Mars* and the *Bellerophon*, had a record at Trafalgar to compare with any, but if the *Aigle* was in fact as well manned as Lucas's *Redoutable*, then she was good indeed, and deserved a victory.

The *Colossus* and *Achille* came next. Some accounts speak of the *Achille* being 'close astern of the *Colossus*, and sailing well', others place them side by side in the column. Whatever may have been their earlier position, they came into action in line of bearing, to starboard of their leaders, and diverging from them. The *Achille* passed close astern of the *Montanez*, luffed up and drove her off, and then pressed on to help the *Belleisle*. On her way she attacked the *Argonaute*, and was herself fired at by the *Achille*. These ships having left her, she engaged the *Berwick*, with whom she was at close quarters for half an hour. The result was success. 'Sent a Lieutenant and men on board the French Ship,' said her log, 'and took possession of her. . . . Received French prisoners on board. Hove overboard sixty-seven butts to make room in the forehold for the prisoners."

The *Colossus* engaged the French *Swiftsure* and the Spanish *Bahama*, both of which struck, the decisive incident in the centre of the French ship being a broadside from the *Orion*. She had left her own line, which was Nelson's, to come to the aid of the hardest pressed ships in Collingwood's column. Both enemy ships were among the prizes which survived, but the *Colossus* herself suffered heavily, with forty killed and a hundred and sixty wounded.

The next two ships should have been the *Dreadnought* and the *Polyphemus*, but they were outsailed by the *Revenge*, a brand new 74 with a name whose battle-honours stretched back to the reign of Elizabeth I. At about 12.30 she opened fire on the *San Ildefonso*, and soon afterwards on the *Achille*, two of whose masts she brought down within a quarter of an hour. But her big battle was with Gravina. His three-decker, the *Principe de Asturias*, 'shot up on my lee quarter,' said Captain Moorsom, while the *Revenge* was enduring a raking fire from elsewhere. 'My friend the Spanish admiral,' continued Moorsom, 'who had been trying hard to dismast me, and succeeded in carrying away all my topsail yards, at last bore up, on the approach of one of our three-decked ships.'

One of the *Revenge*'s seamen recalled that Gravina's ship 'ran her bowsprit over our poop, with a number of her crew on it, and in her fore rigging. Two or three hundred men were ready to follow; but they caught a Tartar, for their design was discovered, and our marines with their small-arms, and the carronnades on the poop, loaded with canister-shot, swept them off so fast that they were glad to sheer off.' In spite of the severity of her encounter with her great antagonist, the *Revenge*, whose losses were heavy, was in good enough trim to form part of the line which prevented the threat from Dumanoir from becoming effective in the later stages of the battle.

The *Defiance* was able to engage about an hour and a quarter after the *Royal Sovereign*. By that time much of her running rigging had been shot away, as she made her approach. She too made at least a brief attack on Gravina, and then set about the *Aigle*, which was by then much the worse for wear, though still game. The *Defiance* 'ran alongside of her, and made fast. Boarded, and got possession of her quarter deck and poop. Struck the French colours, and hoisted English. Her people still firing from the tops, forecastle and lower deck.' This was very much a case of disputed possession, so after five and twenty minutes the boarders were recalled, the ship was cast off, and broadside fire was opened once again. In another half-hour the French called for quarter. 'Ceased firing,' said the *Defiance*'s log: 'out boats, sent a Lieutenant with twenty men to take possession of her.' It had been a gallant resistance, for the *Aigle* had been engaged with at least six ships up and down the lee line. Her hull was battered in every direction, and she had nearly three hundred killed and wounded.

Captain Durham had an extraordinary story to tell afterwards of the first attempt at boarding of the *Aigle*, differing from accounts in the log. A certain Mr Spratt, he said, 'an active young midshipman, took his cutlass between his teeth, called to the boarders to follow, leapt overboard and swam to the *Aigle*, followed by a few men; he got in at the stern port, and was met by some of the crew, who resisted. He succeeded in cutting his way up and hauled down the Frenchman's colours, and in the act of doing so, was shot through the leg.'

He dragged himself to the side of the ship, and holding his bleeding limb over the railing, called out, 'Captain, poor Jack Spratt is done up at last!' Durham managed to warp alongside, and the midshipman was slung on board. Durham was himself by then wounded in the leg and side. Spratt, who was badly hit, refused to have his leg amputated, and the surgeon, feeling that the operation was essential, asked the captain for a written order to authorize him to take the limb off. This was refused, though Durham promised to argue the matter with the midshipman. Spratt held out his other leg, which was a very good one, and said: 'Never; if I lose my leg, where shall I find a match for this?' Spratt was made a lieutenant after the action, and did not in fact lose his leg, but he was seventeen weeks at Gibraltar, and was never able to go to sea again.

After the battle was over Hardy told Durham, by way of comforting him in his wounded state, that Nelson had said to him as they went into action: 'What would poor Sir Robert Calder give to be with us now! Tell your friend Durham he was the most sensible man of the party to stick to his ship.'

The *Dreadnought*, so valuable in fire-power though so poor a sailer, fired her first broadside at Gravina, and later ran alongside Churruca's *San Juan de Nepomuceno*, which struck to her within ten minutes. Then she again attacked Gravina's flagship, which by that time was proceeding towards Cadiz; but she soon found herself outsailed, and broke off her pursuit to help to meet the threat from Dumanoir.

The remaining ships in Collingwood's line, the *Thunderer*, *Defence*, *Polyphemus*, *Swiftsure* and *Prince* had, by comparison with their fellows, light trials and light casualties, the *Prince* having no killed or wounded whatsoever.

The *Thunderer* fired most of her shots at the *San Ildefonso*; the *Defence* was engaged with the French ship *Berwick* as well as the *San Ildefonso*, which struck to her towards the end of the day; the *Swiftsure* did her most useful work in aid of the *Belleisle*, while the *Polyphemus* engaged or pursued a number of ships, though none at very close quarters. As for the powerful *Prince*, handicapped like the *Dreadnought* by her slow speed, she crept upon the scene of violence longing to show her mettle, bent on engaging anything which had life in it.

The *Prince* had had bad luck from the beginning. When the enemy were first signalled, she had been supplying the *Britannia* with water and provisions, and she took some time to put herself in trim for the chase which Nelson ordered. Then on the early morning of the battle she split her fore-topsail, and had scarcely replaced it when the enemy were seen in line, away to leeward. She had a brief encounter with Gravina, raking his *Principe de Asturias* with two broadsides, and at about four o'clock she engaged the *Achille*, brought down her foremast and set her alight. Her boats saved most of the Frenchmen left alive in the ship, some hundred and forty men. Her last act in the battle was to take formal possession of the *Santissima Trinidad*, the principal credit for whose capture belonged to the *Neptune*. Cisneros could yield to a fresh three-decker: the little *Africa* had been quite a different matter.

'How well I remember the *Achille* blowing up,' wrote Hercules Robinson many years later. He had seen the event from the *Euryalus*, and recalled that the frigate 'got hold of a dozen of her men, who were hoisted into the air out of the exploding ship, cursing their fate, tearing their hair, and wiping the gunpowder and salt water from their faces.' Such is human resilience that he was able to add: 'In the evening these same fellows, having got their supper and grog and dry clothes, danced for the amusement of our men, under the half deck.' Nor was the midshipmen's berth in the *Euryalus* without its compensations. Robinson helped in saving a black pig which swam over from the doomed ship: 'and what a glorious supper of pork chops appeared ... instead of our usual refection of cheese, biscuit and salt junk'.

II

As with Collingwood's line, so with Nelson's. It was the leading ships which endured most, and in particular the *Victory* and *Téméraire*. Of the rest – apart from the *Africa* – only the *Britannia* had as many as ten killed, the other ships escaping lightly, thanks to the success of Nelson's plan. Had the van of the Combined Fleet turned earlier, it must have been a different story.

The *Victory*, first to engage, suffered most, but the *Téméraire* ran her close, and no admiral ever had better support than Nelson from Captain Eliab Harvey, a bold gambler, a man of outspoken temper, and a doughty fighter. 'When the *Victory* opened her fire,' said the ship's log, 'immediately put our helm aport to steer clear, and opened our fire on the *Santissima Trinidad* and two ships ahead of her.' These were the French *Neptune* and *Redoutable*. Then 'the action became general'. The fire of the *Téméraire* was decisive in removing all danger from the plucky *Redoutable*, and soon after the Frenchman had ceased resistance, she was free to give the finishing touches to the damaged *Fougueux*, which had drifted over from Collingwood's side.

In his official dispatch on the battle, begun in the *Euryalus* on October 22nd, Collingwood included a story about the *Téméraire* which, though not supported by later evidence, showed the reputation which her prowess had given her. 'A circumstance occurred during the action which so strongly marks the invincible spirit of British seamen that I cannot resist the pleasure I have in making it known to Their Lordships,' wrote Collingwood. 'The *Téméraire* was boarded by accident, or design, by a French ship on one side, and a Spaniard on the other: the contest was vigorous; but in the end the Combined ensigns were torn from the poop, and the British hoisted in their places.' No doubt the scene immediately round the *Victory* was one of glorious confusion, and an observer had made up a picturesque story, which pleased the admiral. There is no likelihood that the *Téméraire* was in fact boarded at any time, though attempts were probably made to do so.

Captain Harvey, in a letter written to his wife after the battle, confirmed that Nelson had given him leave to lead the Weather line 'and to break through the Enemy ... about the 14th ship from the Van', but that afterwards he had annulled this permission by signal. In fact, when going into action the *Téméraire*'s stem almost touched the stern of the *Victory*, 'and,' said Harvey, 'from this for 2 hours we were so nearly engaged that I can give you no other account of this part of the most glorious day's work'.

The ship had, in fact, at least one very near shave, for a 'stink pot', as the sailors called it, 'thrown from the *Redoutable* entered the powder screen on the quarter deck, and caused a destructive explosion on the main-deck below. Had it not been for the presence of mind of the master-at-arms, John Toohig, who was quartered in the light-room, the fire would have communicated to the after-magazine, and probably have occasioned the loss not only of the *Téméraire*, but of the ships near her.'

In the *Neptune*, which was close upon the heels of the *Victory* and *Téméraire*, the scene was recorded in Minutes kept by the signal officer, Lieutenant Andrew Green. These were sent home to his wife at Swanbourne by Captain Fremantle. 'The *Victory* open'd her fire and endeavoured to pass under Stern of the French Admiral in the *Bucentaure*,' said Green. 'The *Redoutable* closed so near, to support his Commander in Chief, that the *Victory* was obliged to lay that ship on board, when both ships paid off before the wind.

'The *Téméraire*, in following gallantly Lord Nelson's ship, fell on the opposite side of the *Redoutable*, from the same cause, and the *Intrépide* alongside the *Téméraire*' (Green was wrong here, for it was the *Fougueux*): 'The four ships lock'd in and on board each other, and their Sterns to us. We put the ship's helm a Starboard and the *Neptune* passed between the *Victory* and *Bucentaure*, with which ship we were warmly engaged (the *Conqueror*'s Jib-boom touching our Taffrail). We passed on to the *Santissima Trinidad*, whose stern was entirely exposed to our fire without being able to return a single shot with effect. At 50 minutes past one observed her Main and Mizen Masts fall overboard, gave three cheers, she then paid off and brought us nearly on her lee Beam, in about a quarter of an hour more, her Foremast fell over her Stern, and shortly after an Officer threw a Union Jack over her Starboard Quarter, hailed the *Neptune* and said they had struck.'

The *Neptune* did not take possession, and for the excellent reason implied in the next sentences in the lieutenant's Minutes. 'The Van of the Enemy now wore and were crossing us apparently with an intent to support their Admirals. The *Conqueror* at this time passed over to windward to engage them. Put our helm a port and fired successfully with six sail of the line that passed to windward, the remaining three going to leeward. Observed the *Leviathan* and another ship closely engaged with two of the Enemy's ships who had bore up and soon after struck.'

The *Leviathan* in fact had engaged the French *Neptune*, and after her encounter with Dumanoir's ships she bore down on the *San Augustin*. After a twenty-minute fight, she carried her by boarding. Maistral in the *Neptune* went off before the wind to attack Collingwood's ships, and was in the final flight to Cadiz, where the ship arrived little damaged, living to fight another day.

As for the *Conqueror*, she at one time engaged both the *Bucentaure* and the *Santissima Trinidad*, but her most useful work was in the later stages of the battle, when she helped to foil Dumanoir. The *Britannia*,* *Ajax* and *Agamemnon* had no close encounters, but, together with the *Orion*, they took part in the *mêlée*, and it was to the *Orion* that the *Intrépide* struck. Captain Codrington, commanding the *Orion*, had first made his name under Howe at the Glorious First of June, when a young officer, and he lived to fly his flag at Navarino as commander-in-chief, a battle which may be said to have been the swan-song of the old sailing-ship of the line. Going into action he reserved his fire until he knew it would be effective, and he found some wry amusement in seeing Berry in the *Agamemnon* blazing away for all he was worth, apparently at friend and foe alike.

The action of the *Spartiate* and the *Minotaur* in foiling Dumanoir has already been described. They were a curious combination, for they had been on opposite sides seven years before, at the Nile, where the *Minotaur* had helped to capture her companion.

William Thorpe, who served in the *Minotaur*, left an interesting account of an address given by her captain, Mansfield, on the eve of going into battle. He turned all the hands up, and told them that they would shortly be in sight of the enemy, at which everyone began to cheer. 'There is every probability of engaging,' he continued, 'and I trust that this day or tomorrow will prove the most glorious our country ever saw. I shall say nothing to you of courage. Our country never produced a coward. For my own part I pledge myself to the officers and ship's company

---

* The *Britannia*, nicknamed "Old Ironsides", was the veteran of the British Fleet, having been launched in 1762, three years before the *Victory*, and a year earlier than the *Defiance*.

never to quit the ship I get alongside of, till either she strikes or sinks, or I sink.

'I have only to recommend silence,' he said, 'and a strict attention to the orders of your officers. Be careful to take good aim, for it is to no purpose to throw shot away. You will now repair to your respective stations, and I will bring the ship into action as soon as possible. *God Save the King!*'

It was a scene that must have been repeated in other ships, as they made their stately way towards the Combined Fleet. Captain Mansfield in fact had his chance of running alongside a Spaniard. She was the *Neptuno*, and she duly struck her flag, being one of the last ships in the battle to do so.

III

Mr Midshipman Badcock, another Trafalgar survivor who lived to achieve his flag, was serving in the *Neptune*. He left one of the best accounts of the appearance of the enemy as the British Fleet approached.

'It was a beautiful sight,' he said, 'when their line was completed, their broadsides turned towards us, showing their iron teeth, and now and then trying the range of a shot to ascertain the distance, that they might, the moment we came within point blank (about six hundred yards), open their fire upon our van ships – no doubt with the hope of dismasting some of our leading vessels before they could close and break their line.

'Some of the enemy's ships were painted like ourselves, with double yellow sides, some with a broad single red or yellow streak, others all black, and the noble *Santissima Trinidada*, with four distinct lines of red, with a white ribbon between them, made her seem a superb man-of-war, which indeed she was. Her appearance was imposing, her head splendidly ornamented with a colossal group of figures, painted white, representing the Holy Trinity from which she took her name.'

Gravina's *Santa Ana* had an enormous effigy of the Virgin's mother, clothed in red, for her figure-head. As a badge of nationality, every French ship bore on her stern a lozenge-shaped escutcheon, painted in three horizontal bands of blue, white and red, and both Cosmao of the *Pluton* and Valdez of the *Neptuno* had three colours flying. Spanish ships each had a large crucifix, and the Frenchmen 'Eagles', dedicated by and to Napoleon.

Accounts of the French and Spanish ships tell much the same story – of gallant resistance, made without any real hope of success; of dreadful carnage and material destruction; of comparatively ineffective gunnery; and of elaborate preparations to board (natural enough in a fleet which contained so many soldiers), which in no case came nearer realization than the *Redoutable*'s brief moment when she might have made a lodgement in the *Victory*, or the *Algéciras*'s when she grappled with the *Tonnant*. It is a story of unrewarded courage, justifying Villeneuve's foreboding, and exemplifying the futility of his training when opposed to men of confident spirit, efficient both in gunnery and seamanship.

The matter is typified in an officer's description of the later stages of the *Bucentaure*'s death-throes. 'The upper decks and gangways, heaped with dead and the wreckage from overhead, presented an appalling spectacle,' he said. 'Amid this scene of disaster Admiral Villeneuve, who from the first had displayed the calmest courage, continued tranquilly pacing up and down the quarter-deck. At length he saw his ship totally dismasted, and no hope of succour coming from any quarter. With bitter sorrow he exclaimed: "The *Bucentaure* has played her part; mine is not yet over." He gave orders for his boat to be got ready at once to take him with his flag on board one of the ships of the van squadron. He still cherished the hope that he might be able, with the fresh ships of the van, to make a supreme effort, and even yet snatch victory from the enemy.

'But the unfortunate admiral's illusion did not last long. Word was soon brought him that his barge, which before the battle had been got ready against this very possibility, had several holes made in it by the enemy's shot, and, as a *finale*, had been crushed to pieces under a mass of fallen spars and rigging. Every single one of the ship's other boats had also been destroyed. On that they hailed across to the *Santissima Trinidada* for them to send a boat, but no reply was made and no boat was sent. Bitterly did Admiral Villeneuve realize his desperate position, and the hard fate that was in store for him. He saw himself imprisoned on board a ship that was unable to defend herself, while a great part of his fleet was in action and fighting hard. He cursed the destiny that had spared him in the midst of all the slaughter round about. Compelled by force of circumstances to think no more about his fleet, he had now only to think of the ship he was in. All he could do now was to see after the lives of the handful of brave men left fighting with him. Humanity forbad him to allow them to be shot down without means of defending themselves. Villeneuve looked away, and allowed the captain of the *Bucentaure* to lower the colours.'

The Allied flagship actually surrendered to an officer of marines, Captain James Atcherley of the *Conqueror*. Israel Pellew, commanding the *Conqueror*, could not spare his first lieutenant, on whom the duty would normally have fallen, and ordered Atcherley to take his place. Atcherley went off with two seamen, and a corporal and two marines. When he gained the *Bucentaure*'s upper deck, and his red coat showed itself on the quarter-deck of the battered vessel, four French officers of rank stepped forward, all bowing and presenting their swords. One was Villeneuve; one was Magendie, the captain of the ship; and one was Major-General Contamine, the senior soldier.

'To whom have I the honour of surrendering?' asked Villeneuve, in English.

'To Captain Pellew of the *Conqueror*.'

'I am glad to have struck to the fortunate Sir Edward Pellew.'

'It is his brother, sir,' said Atcherley.

'His brother! What, are there two of them!' exclaimed Villeneuve. '*Helas!*'

'*Fortune de la guerre*,' said Magendie, as he became a prisoner of war for the third time. All the Frenchmen knew of Sir Edward Pellew, who, when in command of a frigate, had driven the battleship *Droits de l'Homme* ashore in 1797. The younger brother was, it seemed, equally formidable.

Atcherley suggested that the swords of such senior officers should be handed to someone of higher rank than himself. He then went below to secure the magazines, passing through scenes of horror. 'The dead, thrown back as they fell, lay along the middle of the decks in heaps,' he said, 'and the shot, passing through, had frightfully mangled the bodies. . . . An extraordinary proportion had lost their heads. A raking shot, which entered the lower deck, had glanced along the beams and through the thickest of the people, and a French officer declared that this shot alone had killed or disabled nearly forty men.'

The marine officer locked up the magazines, and put the keys in his pocket, he posted his two marines as sentries at the doors of the admiral's and flag-captain's cabins and then, returning on deck, conducted Villeneuve, Magendie and Prigny down the side into his little boat, which went off in search of the *Conqueror*. Pellew, however, had ranged ahead to engage another opponent, and as Atcherley could not see her in the smoke, the Frenchmen were taken to the nearest British ship, which happened to be the *Mars*, the *Conqueror*'s sister-ship. And so it was that, for the second time, Villeneuve gave himself into the charge of a junior officer, Captain Duff having been killed about an hour before.

Nelson's Memorandum had enjoined that 'every effort must be made to capture their Commander-in-Chief'. His orders had now been obeyed, and for such direction as the Allied Fleet could receive for the rest of the battle, they would have to look to Admiral Gravina, who was hard pressed himself, and away from the centre of the fighting. Villeneuve told Blackwood later that he thought 'such a victory and in circumstances so disadvantageous to the attack never was achieved before', and that he could, 'scarcely credit it, and his despair and grief exceeds anything I ever saw. To resist such an attack, surrounded as Lord Nelson was, was vain,' he said, and none of his subordinates would have disagreed with him, though their luck in the encounter varied greatly.

Admiral Alava's flagship, the *Santa Ana*, had better fortune than the *Bucentaure*, though only relatively, and chiefly because she had consistent support. According to the French captain Maistral of the *Neptune*, she did not at first put up a fight against the *Royal Sovereign* which in any way corresponded to her strength. Maistral's ship was ahead of the *Santa Ana* in the Allied line, and he turned to give her help, much as the *Redoutable* had done in the case of the *Bucentaure*, though less closely. As he approached, Maistral 'observed that several men were hiding themselves outside the ship on the opposite side to the enemy. It was therefore essential to assist this vessel in her defence, that she might not fall into the hands of the enemy from the very first shots.' Maistral was successful in preventing the *Santa Ana* from striking until 2.20 in the afternoon. Collingwood then sent Blackwood over, to convey Admiral Alava to the *Euryalus*, but he was told that Alava was on the point of death, and he returned only with the Spanish flag-captain.

That officer had already been to the *Royal Sovereign* to

deliver his sword, and had asked one of the sailors the name of the ship to which he had struck. When told that it was the *Royal Sovereign* he replied in broken English, patting one of the guns: 'I think she should be called the Royal Devil!'

Blackwood had brought over a sword to Collingwood, which he had understood to be Alava's, but which was in fact that of Francisco Riquelme, the senior unwounded lieutenant. Alava was lying below unconscious, though his wound was not in fact as grave as had at first appeared. The *Santa Ana* was recaptured during the storm which followed the battle, with Alava still on board, and a courteous correspondence between him and Collingwood followed, Alava insisting that he had in fact never surrendered. As his nephew, who was serving with Gravina in the *Principe de Asturias*, survived to take service with the Spanish army against France in the Peninsular War, and was ADC to Wellington at Waterloo, later becoming Spanish Ambassador in London, Collingwood's tacit acceptance of the Admiral's statement was in the long run indirectly rewarded, though he continued to believe that Alava's own conduct was wrong. Years later, writing from Minorca to Admiral Purvis about the Spanish ships which were then allied with his own, Collingwood said: 'Place no confidence in Alava nor in any person belonging to the ships; I have good reason for it: but carefully conceal any suspicion of their loyalty.' Collingwood did not forget.

Gravina's wound was much more serious, and in fact he died from its effects some weeks after the battle. He fought his ship with gallantry, and although it was he who, after the capture of Villeneuve, gave the signal for the Combined Fleet to rally and to make for Cadiz, this was a sensible course, considering how the day was going, and it was one which had the full concurrence of Cosmao of the *Pluton*, the ablest among the uncaptured French officers. Cosmao, like Nelson, saw that a storm was likely to blow up from the west, and that he might have a good opportunity to make a sortie later from Cadiz, and even to recapture some of the prizes lost to the British. Some writers have blamed his conduct as pusillanimous. Events showed that he was a wise man, and a realist. With a little better luck, his decision might have been well rewarded. As it happened, it only helped to make a decisive victory still more complete.

Gravina had with him, in addition to his own flagship, the French *Neptune*, the *Pluton* and the *San Leandro*. On his way to Cadiz he picked up the *San Justo*, *Argonaute*, *Montanez* and *Indomptable* from the centre, and the *Heros*, *Rayo* and *San Francisco* from the van, eleven ships in all. Four more, the *Formidable*, *Duguay-Trouin*, *Mont Blanc* and *Scipion* had withdrawn south-westward with Dumanoir. The rest remained in British hands, or were 'driving about, perfect wrecks, at the mercy of the waves', to quote the *Gibraltar Chronicle*.

IV

'Partial firing continued until 4.30,' ran the battle entry in the *Victory*'s log, 'when a victory having been reported to the Right Honourable Lord Viscount Nelson, KB and Commander-in-Chief, he then died of his wound.'

The final scene in Nelson's life was recorded by Dr Beatty in an account which, by reason of its directness and authenticity, demands to be quoted exactly as he wrote it.

With the handkerchief still across his face, Nelson was carried to the orlop deck of the *Victory* by Serjeant Secker and his party.

'Several wounded officers and about forty men were likewise carried to the Surgeon for assistance just at this time,' said Beatty, 'and some others had breathed their last during their conveyance below. Among the latter were Lieutenant William Andrew Ram and Mr Whipple, Captain's clerk. The Surgeon had just examined these two officers, and found that they were dead, when his attention was arrested by several of the wounded calling to him, "Mr Beatty, Lord Nelson is here; Mr Beatty, the Admiral is wounded."

'The Surgeon now, on looking round, saw the handkerchief fall from his Lordship's face; when the stars on his coat, which also had been covered by it, appeared. Mr Burke, the Purser, and the Surgeon, ran immediately to the assistance of his Lordship, and took him from the arms of the Seamen who had carried him below. In conveying him to one of the Midshipmen's berths, they stumbled, but recovered themselves without falling. Lord Nelson then inquired who were supporting him; and when the Surgeon informed him, his Lordship replied, "Ah, Mr Beatty, you can do nothing for me. I have but a short time to live: my back is shot through."

'The Surgeon said he "hoped the wound was not so dangerous as his Lordship imagined, and that he might still survive long to enjoy his glorious victory."

'The Reverend Doctor Scott, who had been absent in another part of the cockpit administering lemonade to the wounded, now came instantly to his Lordship; and in his anguish of grief wrung his hands, and said: "Alas, Beatty, how prophetic you were!" alluding to the apprehensions expressed by the Surgeon for his Lordship's safety, previous to the battle.

'His Lordship was laid upon a bed, stripped of his clothes, and covered with a sheet. While this was effecting, he said to Dr Scott, "Doctor, I told you so; Doctor, I am gone!" and after a short pause, he added in a low voice, "I have to leave Lady Hamilton and my adopted daughter Horatia, as a legacy to my Country."

'The Surgeon then examined the wound, assuring his Lordship that he would not put him to much pain in endeavouring to discover the course of the ball; which he soon found had penetrated deep into the chest, and had probably lodged in the spine.

'This being explained to his Lordship, he replied he "was confident his back was shot through".

'The back was then examined externally, but without any injury being perceived; on which his Lordship was requested by the Surgeon to make him acquainted with all his sensations.

'He replied, that he felt a gush of blood every minute within his breast: that he had no feeling in the lower part of his body: and that his breathing was difficult, and attended with very severe pain about that part of the spine where he was confident that the ball had struck; "for," said he, "I felt it break my back".

'These symptoms, but more particularly the gush of blood which his Lordship complained of, together with the state of his pulse, indicated to the Surgeon the hopeless situation of the case; but till after the victory was ascertained and announced to his Lordship, the true nature of his wound was concealed by the Surgeon from all on board, except only Captain Hardy, Doctor Scott, Mr Burke and Messrs Smith and Westemburg, the Assistant-Surgeons.

'The *Victory*'s crew cheered whenever they observed an Enemy's Ship surrender. On one of these occasions, Lord Nelson anxiously inquired what was the cause of it; when Lieutenant Pasco, who lay wounded at some distance from his Lordship, raised himself up, and told him that another Ship had struck: which appeared to give him much satisfaction.

'He now felt an ardent thirst; and frequently called for drink, and to be fanned with paper, making use of these words: "Fan, fan," and "Drink, drink." This he continued to repeat, when he wished for drink or the refreshment of cool air, till a very few minutes before he expired. Lemonade, and wine and water, were given to him occasionally.

'He evinced great solicitude for the event of the battle,

and fears for the safety of his friend Captain Hardy. Doctor Scott and Mr Burke used every argument they could suggest to relieve his anxiety. Mr Burke told him "the Enemy were decisively defeated, and that he hoped his Lordship would still live to be himself the bearer of the joyful tidings to his Country".

'He replied, "It is nonsense, Mr Burke, to suppose I can live: my sufferings are great, but they will all be soon over."

'Dr Scott entreated his Lordship not to despair of living, and said he "trusted that Divine Providence would restore him once more to his dear Country and friends."

' "Ah, Doctor!" replied his Lordship, "it is all over; it is all over."

'Many messages were sent to Captain Hardy by the Surgeon, requesting his attendance on his Lordship, who became impatient to see him, and often exclaimed: "Will no one bring Hardy to me? He must be killed: he is surely destroyed."

'The Captain's Aide-de-camp, Mr Bulkeley, now came below, and stated that "circumstances respecting the Fleet required Captain Hardy's presence on deck, but that he would avail himself of the first favourable moment to visit his Lordship".

'On hearing him deliver this message to the Surgeon, his Lordship inquired who had brought it.

'Mr Burke answered: "It is Mr Bulkeley, my Lord."

' "It is his voice," replied his Lordship; he then said to the young gentleman, "Remember me to your father."

'An hour and ten minutes however elapsed, from the time of his Lordship's being wounded, before Captain Hardy's first subsequent interview with him; the particulars of which are nearly as follow. They shook hands affectionately, and Lord Nelson said: "Well, Hardy, how goes the battle? How goes the day with us?"

' "Very well, my Lord," replied Captain Hardy. "We

have got twelve or fourteen of the Enemy's Ships in our possession; but five of their van have tacked, and show an intention of bearing down upon the *Victory*. I have, therefore, called two or three of our fresh ships round us, and have no doubt of giving them a drubbing."

' "I hope," said his Lordship, "none of *our* Ships have struck, Hardy?"

' "No, my Lord," replied Captain Hardy; "there is no fear of that."

'Lord Nelson then said: "I am a dead man, Hardy. I am going fast; it will be all over with me soon. Come nearer to me. Pray let my dear Lady Hamilton have my hair, and all other things belonging to me."

'Mr Burke was about to withdraw at the commencement of this conversation; but his Lordship, perceiving his intention, desired he would remain. Captain Hardy observed, that he "hoped Mr Beatty could yet hold out some prospect of life".

' "Oh, no," answered his Lordship, "it is impossible. My back is shot through. Beatty will tell you so."

'Captain Hardy then returned on deck, and at parting shook hands again with his revered friend and Commander.

'His Lordship now requested the Surgeon, who had been previously absent a short time attending Mr Rivers (a midshipman who lost a leg), to return to the wounded and give his assistance to such of them as he could be useful to; "for," said he, "you can do nothing for me".

'The Surgeon assured him that the Assistant-Surgeons were doing everything that could be effected for those unfortunate men; but on his Lordship's several times repeating his injunctions to that purpose, he left him, surrounded by Dr Scott, Mr Burke and two of his Lordship's domestics.

'After the Surgeon had been absent a few minutes attending Lieutenants Peake and Reeves of the Marines, who were wounded, he was called by Doctor Scott to his

Lordship, who said: "Ah, Mr Beatty! I have sent for you to say, what I forgot to tell you before, that all power of motion and feeling below my breast are gone; and *you*", continued he, "very well *know* I can live but a short time."

'The emphatic manner in which he pronounced these last words, left no doubt in the Surgeon's mind, that he adverted to the case of a man who had some months before received a mortal injury of the spine on board the *Victory*, and had laboured under similar privations of sense and muscular motion. The case had made a great impression on Lord Nelson; he was anxious to know the cause of such symptoms, which was accordingly explained to him; and he now appeared to apply the situation and fate of this man to himself.

'The Surgeon answered: "My Lord, you told me so before"; but he now examined the extremities, to ascertain the fact, when his Lordship said, "Ah, Beatty! I am too certain of it; Scott and Burke have tried it already. *You know* I am gone."

'The Surgeon replied: "My Lord, unhappily for our Country, nothing can be done for you"; and having made this declaration he was so much affected that he turned round and withdrew a few steps to conceal his emotions.

'His Lordship said: "I know it. I feel something rising in my breast," putting his hand on his left side, "which tells me I am gone."

'Drink was recommended liberally, and Doctor Scott and Mr Burke fanned him with paper. He often exclaimed: "God be praised, I have done my duty"; and upon the Surgeon's inquiring whether his pain was still very great, he declared, "it continued so very severe, that he wished he was dead. Yet", said he in a lower voice, "one would like to live a little longer, too"; and after a pause of a few minutes, he added in the same tone: "What would become of poor Lady Hamilton, if she knew my situation?"

'The Surgeon, finding it impossible to render his Lordship any further assistance, left him, to attend Lieutenant Bligh, Messrs Smith and Westphal, Midshipmen, and some Seamen, recently wounded.

'Captain Hardy now came to the cockpit to see his Lordship a second time, which was after an interval of about fifty minutes from the conclusion of his first visit. Before he quitted the deck, he sent Lieutenant Hills to acquaint Admiral Collingwood with the lamentable circumstance of Lord Nelson's being wounded.

'Lord Nelson and Captain Hardy shook hands again; and while the Captain retained his Lordship's hand, he congratulated him, even in the arms of death, on his brilliant victory, "which", said he, "was complete; though he did not know how many of the Enemy were captured, as it was impossible to perceive every Ship distinctly. He was certain, however, of fourteen or fifteen having surrendered."

'His Lordship answered: "That is well, but I bargained for twenty"; and then emphatically exclaimed: "*Anchor*, Hardy, *anchor!*"

'To this the Captain replied: "I suppose, my Lord, Admiral Collingwood will now take upon himself the direction of affairs."

' "Not while I live, I hope, Hardy!" cried the dying Chief, and at that moment endeavoured ineffectually to raise himself from the bed. "No," added he; "do *you* anchor, Hardy."

'Captain Hardy then said, "Shall *we* make the signal, Sir?"

' "Yes," answered his Lordship, "for if I live, I'll anchor."

'The energetic manner in which he uttered these his last orders to Captain Hardy, accompanied with his efforts to raise himself, evinced his determination never to resign the Command while he retained the exercise of his transcendent faculties, and that he expected Captain Hardy still to carry into effect the suggestions of his exalted mind; a sense of his duty overcoming the pains of death.

'He then told Captain Hardy he "felt that in a few minutes he should be no more"; adding in a low tone: "Don't throw me overboard, Hardy."

'The Captain answered: "Oh no, certainly not."

' "Then," replied his Lordship, "you know what to do; and," continued he, "take care of my dear Lady Hamilton, Hardy. Take care of poor Lady Hamilton. Kiss me, Hardy."

'The Captain now knelt down and kissed his cheek, when his Lordship said: "Now I am satisfied. Thank God, I have done my duty."

'Captain Hardy stood for a minute or two in silent contemplation. He knelt down again, and kissed his Lordship's forehead.

'His Lordship said: "Who is that?"

'The Captain answered: "It is Hardy" to which his Lordship replied: "God bless you, Hardy!"

'After this affecting scene Captain Hardy withdrew, and returned to the quarter-deck, having spent about eight minutes in this his last interview with his dying friend.

'Lord Nelson now desired Mr Chevalier, his Steward, to turn him upon his right side, which being effected, his Lordship said: "I wish I had not left the deck, for I shall soon be gone."

'He afterwards became very low; his breathing was oppressed, and his voice faint. He said to Doctor Scott: "Doctor, I have not been a *great* sinner", and after a short pause, "*Remember*, that I leave Lady Hamilton and my Daughter Horatia as a legacy to my Country: and," added he, "never forget Horatia."

'His thirst now increased, and he called for "drink, drink", "fan, fan" and "rub, rub", addressing himself in the last case to Doctor Scott, who had been rubbing his

Lordhip's breast with his hand, from which he found some relief. These words he spoke in a very rapid manner, which rendered his articulation difficult: but he every now and then, with evident increase of pain, made a greater effort with his vocal powers, and pronounced distinctly these last words: "Thank God, I have done my duty"; and this great sentiment he continued to repeat so long as he was able to give it utterance.

'His Lordship became speechless in about fifteen minutes after Captain Hardy left him. Doctor Scott and Mr Burke, who had all along sustained the bed under his shoulders (which raised him in nearly a semi-recumbent posture, the only one that was supportable to him), forebore to disturb him by speaking to him; and when he had remained speechless about five minutes, his Lordship's Steward went to the Surgeon, who had been a short time occupied with the wounded in another part of the cockpit, and stated his apprehensions that his Lordship was dying.

'The Surgeon immediately repaired to him and found him on the verge of dissolution. He knelt down by his side and took up his hand, which was cold, and the pulse gone from the wrist. On the Surgeon's feeling his forehead, which was likewise cold, his Lordship opened his eyes, looked up, and shut them again.

'The Surgeon again left him and returned to the wounded who required his assistance, but was not absent five minutes before the Steward announced to him that he "believed his Lordship had expired".

'The Surgeon returned and found that the report was but too well founded; his Lordship had breathed his last, at thirty minutes past four o'clock, at which period Doctor Scott was in the act of rubbing his Lordship's breast, and Mr Burke supporting the bed under his shoulders.

'From the time of his Lordship's being wounded till his death, a period of about two hours and forty-five minutes elapsed (or perhaps half an hour more); but a knowledge of the decisive victory which was gained he acquired of Captain Hardy within the first hour and a quarter of this period. A partial cannonade, however, was still maintained, in consequence of the Enemy's running Ships passing the British at different points; and the last distant guns which were fired at their Van Ships that were making off, were heard a minute or two before his Lordship expired.'

6

The Storm

THE DARKNESS OF THE NIGHT after the battle
hid scenes of confusion and distress. No Admiral's light
burnt in the *Victory*, and Collingwood could not for some
time hope to get his ships into regular order, though discipline was unimpaired. It soon became clear that some vessels would have difficulty in keeping afloat. In a material
sense, those which, battered as they were, had found refuge
in Cadiz, were best off. Among the rest out at sea, victors
and vanquished, the work of immediate repair, of tending
the wounded, of disposing of the dead, and above all of incessant work at the pumps, to keep leaks within control,
engaged the attention and energies of every able-bodied
survivor. And it proved, soon enough, that Nelson had been
right. The earlier swell from the westward had been the
portent of a coming storm. The wind increased throughout
the hours of darkness, and it continued, rising to gale force,
for several days.

Most ships were short-handed, the British not only
through casualties, but because men were detached to the
prizes; the vanquished because the larger proportion of
their people were demoralized, and incapable of sustained
work. A few captains, remembering Nelson's signal to prepare to anchor, now obeyed it. Those who did so, profited.
Of those who did not, some were incapable of carrying out
the instruction owing to damage to anchors and cables,
while others considered themselves better off with more sea-
room. These made their way, or were towed, like the *Royal
Sovereign*, farther from the shoals which were to leeward.

Conditions in the prizes were always difficult. In the
case of ships which had been severely handled, they were

sometimes shocking. Mr Midshipman Badcock, for instance, was sent from the *Neptune* to the *Santissima Trinidad*, which everyone in the British fleet, from Collingwood downward, longed to see their own. The first job to be done on board the great ship was the grisly one of heaving corpses overboard. There were over two hundred killed, and the Spaniards were in no state to help. Badcock then had to see to the securing of prisoners, including many soldiers, and to get as many as possible away to British ships. Below, he found the beams covered with blood, the decks still slippery, and the after part of the vessel almost choked with wounded, many armless or legless, none of whom had been properly attended. Nor was there any prospect of giving them immediate relief.

The *Minotaur*'s experience was typical of those ships, relatively little damaged, which were best able to supply prize parties. Towards the close of day she sent a lieutenant of marines with sixty-eight men to the Spanish *Neptuno*. They reached her at half-past five, sending the *Neptuno*'s first lieutenant back to their own ship, to deliver his dead captain's sword.

The prisoners, fire-arms and ammunition were duly secured, the magazines locked, after which the British discovered that the ship was very leaky, and that there was no shot-plug on board. Men were sent over to the *Minotaur* for the essential materials, and the party set about stopping the worst holes. Prisoners were set to work at the pumps, for the *Neptuno* had five foot of water in the hold, and this was increasing.

On the morning of the 22nd the party began clearing away wreckage, after which the *Minotaur* took the *Neptuno* in tow. But the wind rose, the hawser broke, and the Spaniard was once again left to the care of her prize party.

The *San Juan de Nepomuceno*, which had actually struck to the *Dreadnought*, was left to the *Tonnant* to secure. The *Tonnant*'s captain sent Lieutenant Clements to board her, but by that time, so the lieutenant recorded, 'there was no available boat but what was shot. However,' he continued, 'I was told I must try, and so I went away in the jolly-boat with two men. I had not gone above a quarter of the way, when we swamped.' Clements could not swim, but the two men held him up, one of them being a Negro. The trio were at length fished out of the water, and returned to comparative safety. Similar incidents occurred in other ships. Boats set out, were found to be damaged, and their people suffered. But eventually prize crews were in possession of most of the surrendered vessels, though one of them, the *Algéciras*, was retaken by her own men, and brought into Cadiz, adding another unit to the surviving force.

Again, it was the *Tonnant* that was concerned. She had sent a lieutenant and fifty men as prize crew, and they had under hatches in the hold two hundred and seventy French officers and men. At dawn on October 22nd the ship had drifted too far inshore to hope for help from the British fleet, and as the morning advanced, they came close to the rocks. Lieutenant Bennett and his men were too few to guard the prisoners as well as to rig jury-masts, which alone could save the ship. As the only chance for all on board, the lieutenant had the hatches taken off, and the Frenchmen were set free. They swarmed on deck and, headed by one of their officers, Lieutenant de la Bretonnière – whose action made his name in the French Navy, and eventually brought him his flag – at once made it clear to Bennett that they resumed possession of the ship, and that if the British resisted, they would be thrown overboard. If, on the other hand, the prize crew helped to save the ship, they were promised their liberty. In the circumstances, Bennett agreed, and British and French, working together, succeeded in getting up three topgallant masts, and so reached port.

Among the prisoners was a woman, Jeanette of the

Achille. Her story was told by a lieutenant of the *Revenge*. 'On the morning after the action I had charge of the deck,' he said, 'the other officers and crew being at breakfast, when a boat-load of prisoners of war came alongside, all of whom, with one exception, were in the costume of Adam. The exception was apparently a youth, but clothed in an old jacket and trousers, with a dingy handkerchief tied round the head, and exhibiting a face begrimed with smoke and dirt, without shoes, stockings or shirt, and looking the picture of misery and despair.

'The appearance of this person at once attracted my attention, and on asking some questions I was answered that the prisoner was a woman. It was sufficient to know this, and I lost no time in introducing her to my mess-mates, as a female requiring their compassionate attention. The poor creature was almost famishing with hunger, having tasted nothing for four and twenty hours, consequently she required no persuasion to partake of the breakfast upon the table. I then gave her up my cabin, and made a collection of all the articles which could be procured to enable her to complete a more suitable wardrobe.

'One of the lieutenants gave her a piece of sprigged blue muslin, which he had obtained from a Spanish prize, and two new checked shirts were supplied by the purser; these, with a purser's blanket, and my ditty bag, which contained needles, thread, etc., being placed at her disposal she, in a short time, appeared in a very different, and much more becoming costume. Being a dressmaker, she had made herself a sort of a jacket, after the Flemish fashion, and the purser's shirts had been transformed into an outer-petticoat; she had a silk handkerchief tastily tied over her head, and another thrown round her shoulders: white stockings and a pair of the chaplain's shoes were on her feet, and altogether our guest, which we unanimously voted her, appeared a very interesting young woman.'

Jeanette's quick recovery was astonishing, considering

what she had been through. In action, she had been stationed in the passage to the fore magazine, to help in handing up the powder. When firing ceased, she went in search of her husband, but found that all the ladders to the upper decks had by that time been shot away. Then there came the alarm of fire, and poor Jeanette wandered to and fro among the dead and dying, while the flames raged above, and guns from the main deck began to fall through the burnt planks. Her only possible refuge was by now outside, and she scrambled out of the gun-room port 'and, by the help of the rudder-chains, reached the back of the rudder, where she remained some time, praying the ship might blow up, and put an end to her misery'.

'At length,' so she told her captors, 'the lead which lined the rudder-trunk began to melt, and to fall upon her, and her only means of avoiding this was to leap overboard.' First she found a lump of cork, which kept her up for some time, and then a man, swimming near, gave her a piece of plank, which she placed under her arms, and this supported her until she was picked up. About four days later, she heard that her husband had also been rescued, and when she eventually landed at Gibraltar, it was with a small purse of dollars given her by the *Revenge*'s officers. This was one instance among many when Nelson's wish that 'humanity after victory' should be 'the predominant feature in the British Fleet', was fulfilled to the letter.

Another French woman from the *Achille* was picked up by the *Britannia*. She had been dressed in the costume of a harlequin, and was given a large cotton dressing-gown by the lieutenant of marines. It is also certain that there were one or two women on board the British ships, though no record of their adventures appears to have survived. It had been so at the Glorious First of June, when a woman in HMS *Tremendous* had recently become a mother. Her son, Daniel Tremendous Mackenzie, duly received the Naval General Service medal, with the appropriate clasp, when it was issued in 1848, by which time he was an ageing man. Two women who were present at the Nile were refused this medal, but, with the illogicality which sometimes pervades such matters, it was allowed to Jane Townsend, who was on board the *Defiance* at Trafalgar.

Among the curiosities of the time was the convention that frigates and other vessels which by reason of their size were not eligible to 'lie in the line of battle', were usually free from attack, in a large-scale action, by the big ships, though it was not one which was always strictly observed. At Trafalgar, the British frigates played a notable part throughout, not only in repeating signals, which was one of their normal duties, but in helping damaged ships. On the other hand the frigates of the Combined Fleet, the *Cornélie, Hermione, Hortense, Rhin* and *Thémis*, and the brigs *Argus* and *Furet*, did far less. They kept to leeward during the action, in which position they could see little but smoke and general confusion, and their signalling left much to be desired, though they helped in the later stages of the battle. For instance, it was the *Thémis* that towed Gravina's *Principe de Asturias* into Cadiz, while under Captain Cosmao's orders they were to be given their opportunity in the later sortie.

II

On October 22nd there was a strong wind all day, with squalls. The weather was mainly from the south, which was of help in keeping prizes from driving ashore, but was foul for Gibraltar, where the British wished to take them. Next day the wind increased, and in the afternoon, conditions favouring his leaving Cadiz, Cosmao made his foray. His idea was both to rescue the prizes which he could see tossing about in the bay, and to prove that, even if defeated, there was yet a high spirit among the French and Spanish survivors. He deserved better luck than befell him. He had three French and two Spanish ships of the line, the *Pluton*, *Indomptable*, *Neptune*, *Rayo* and *San Francisco de Asis*, together with a number of frigates and brigs. Some of the battleships were seriously damaged, but Cosmao thought that they could hold off any counter-attack which Collingwood could launch before nightfall, while the frigates and brigs, which were undamaged and handy, could show their qualities in boarding and towing.

He had one success. The *Santa Ana*, with Alava on board, was retaken, the *Thunderer* first having time to withdraw her prize crew. He might well have had another, for in the Spanish *Neptuno* the ship's company, seeing what was happening, turned on the *Minotaur*'s party, and helped one of the French frigates to secure a tow. Even so, the *Neptuno* was soon in trouble, and she drove ashore off Rota, British and Spanish working hard until the last to save themselves and the ship. Otherwise, all was disaster. Collingwood soon called up a number of 74's to drive Cosmao back, and the Frenchman actually lost no less than three of his main force. The *Indomptable* blundered across to Rota, and was wrecked near the *Neptuno*, with the loss of all hands. The *San Francisco de Asis* parted her cables after anchoring, and drove ashore near one of the Cadiz forts, while the three-decked *Rayo*, unable to regain harbour, rolled her masts out off San Luca, and had to surrender at discretion to the *Donegal*, Captain Sir Pulteney Malcolm. This officer, fresh from Gibraltar, not only had the mortification of missing Trafalgar, but even his unexpected prize was lost to him later, by weather.

III

Cosmao's ineffective gallantry was not popular in Cadiz. The citizens had seen two more of their own nation's ships perish off their shore, and even the rescue of Alava was imperfect compensation. But what Cosmao could not accomplish in denying the victors the fruits of their skill, the elements took in their stride. The *Redoutable* sank while in tow of the *Swiftsure*, five of whose men, with thirteen from the *Téméraire*, went down with her; four others were wrecked, the *Berwick*, *Aigle*, *Bucentaure* and *Fougueux*, the *Bucentaure* taking part of her own crew, and the *Fougueux* all her own men, as well as thirty from the *Téméraire*. And on October 24th, as the weather still proved furious, Collingwood gave the order to 'Quit and withdraw men from prizes after having destroyed or disabled them.'

This was a sad moment for the Fleet, even though, as Collingwood said, 'I can only say that in my life I never saw such exertions as were made to save those Ships; and would rather fight another Battle, than pass such a week as followed it.' Officers and men were robbed of the visible signs of their triumph; still more important to them (since that triumph needed no trophies to establish its extent) they saw their prize-money vanish beneath the waves.

First there was the task of removing not merely the prize-crews, but the remaining prisoners, and particularly the wounded. Then the demolition and fire parties set to work. Saddest perhaps was the case of the *Santissima Trinidad*. Badcock noted that she was built of cedar, and thought that the order to abandon her was premature. But it was with the greatest difficulty that she had been kept afloat so long, and already tired men worked themselves to exhaustion in moving her sick. Even when she finally disappeared, she was thought to have carried at least some living men with her, though her cat was one of the earlier rescues.

In the end, the four ships which were brought to Gibraltar, the French *Swiftsure*, the Spanish *Bahama*, *San Ildefonso* and the *San Juan de Nepomuceno*, were a raddled and undistinguishable lot, though in fact the number of prizes was to be increased in an unexpected way, in an action which took its place as a pendant to the main battles.

At Cadiz, when parties landed from the British fleet (mainly survivors from prize crews which had been wrecked), nothing could have exceeded the kindness of the Spaniards, from the Governor to the meekest nursing sister. They had little to offer, but everything they had was given unstintingly, and with unfailing courtesy. Every account speaks of the kindly spirit which continued between the Spanish and the British.

Hercules Robinson was sent in later with his captain, Blackwood, to arrange an exchange of prisoners, Blackwood 'rather short, but of extraordinary strength and finely made, well set up, a fresh complexion and small hands and feet'. The Spaniards were impressed with his bearing and his fine uniform 'a gold-laced cocked hat, gold-laced coat and epaulettes, white pantaloons and Hessian boots, a light crooked sabre, and a great shirt frill'. Robinson, as Blackwood's aide-de-camp, found himself enjoying pineapple and old sherry at the house of the Governor, the Marquis of Solano.

Codrington of the *Orion* recorded one case in which the master of a boarding-party, landing at Cadiz in a boat, was received by a carriage 'backed into the water for him to step into; all sorts of cordials and confectionery were placed in the carriage for him, and clean linen, bed, etc., prepared for him at a lodging on shore; added to which the women and priests provided him with delicacies of all sorts as the carriage passed along the streets'. In short, he says, 'and with very great truth, that had he been wrecked in any part of England he would never have received one-half the attention which he did from these poor Spaniards, whose friends we had just destroyed in such numbers; but, I must add, the survivors amongst whom we had been at the greatest pains and risks in saving from the jaws of death'.

Formerly allies, British and Spanish would end the long

war on the same side, and their enmity was never deep throughout the years when Spain was politically linked with France. The Spaniards were monarchist and religious – so, in their differing ways, were the British. With the French it was different. They were prickly allies, and, so the Spaniards thought, ungenerous foes. Most of them had at one time publicly professed atheism, and although they now boasted an Emperor, and made a great show of the allegiance to the new dynasty, it was as a soldier that Napoleon had made his name, and his action in throwing away both his own fleet and that of his allies did not endear him to the victims.

When Rosily at last arrived from Madrid on his master's business, he found cold comfort, and a destroyed command. He must privately have blessed the day that Villeneuve decided to put to sea without him. His mission now devolved into holding inquiries and writing reports, an activity which was familiar to him. He could blame the absent Villeneuve to his heart's content, secure in the knowledge that he himself would be spared that unhappy man's successive dilemmas.

Collingwood, in his clear and graceful way, summed up the whole matter in a letter to Admiral Sir Peter Parker, written from the *Queen*, off Cadiz, within eleven days of the battle. It had been Parker who, many years before, had 'made' both him and Nelson, giving them command of frigates in the West Indies during the War of American Independence. Collingwood and Nelson had in their turn been in a position to help younger members of Parker's family, which they did with faithful gratitude.

'You will have seen from the public accounts that we have fought a great Battle,' said Collingwood, 'and had it not been for the fall of our noble friend, who was indeed the glory of England and the admiration of all who ever saw him in Battle, your pleasure would have been perfect – that two of your own pupils, raised under your eye, and cherished by your kindness, should render such Service to their Country as I hope this Battle, in its effect, will be.'

'. . . It was a severe Action, no dodging or manoeuvring. They formed their line with nicety, and awaited our attack with great composure, nor did they fire a gun until we were close to them, we began first.'

Not all accounts agree with Collingwood's on this point, but those are his words.

'. . . our Ships were fought with a degree of gallantry that would have warmed your heart. Everybody exerted themselves, and a glorious day was made of it.'

'People who cannot comprehend how complicated an affair a Battle at sea is, and who judge of an Officer's conduct by the number of sufferers in his Ship, often do him a wrong. Though there will appear great differences in the loss of men, all did admirably well; and the conclusion was grand beyond description; eighteen hulks of the Enemy lying among the British Fleet without a stick standing, and the French *Achille* burning. But we were close to the rocks of Trafalgar, and when I made the signal for anchoring, many Ships had their cables shot, and not an anchor ready. Providence did for us what no human effort could have done, the wind shifted a few points and we drifted off the land.

'The storm being violent, and many of our Ships in most perilous situations, I found it necessary to order the captures, all without masts, some without rudders, and many half full of water, to be destroyed, except such as were in better plight; for my object was their ruin and not what might be made of them.'

Collingwood's words, particularly the last sentence,

might have been written by his dead friend. Though so differing in temperament, they were at one in their purpose. 'What might be made of them' proved in fact little enough, to most of the Fleet. When the Prize Money and Grant were at last distributed, there were five classes of share. The highest amounted to a total of £3,362 7s. 6d.; which was no despicable award; then there was a great drop to £225 11s.; the third and fourth classes were £148 12s. and £27 respectively; while the share of an ordinary seaman was the princely sum of £6 10s. In the case of those wounded, the Committee of Lloyd's added sums ranging from £100 to severely wounded lieutenants, to £10 to slightly wounded seamen, which gave an unfair advantage to those ships which had made the most of their casualties.

Prize was one thing, credit another. However severe his outward aspect (and Collingwood never received from his captains half the affection which Nelson could summon at once, and keep throughout their lives), Collingwood was like Nelson in the generosity of his praise to dead and living alike. Captain Durham of the *Defiance* had an excellent example of the trait when he went to call on Collingwood in the *Euryalus* after the action. As so often, Collingwood was writing in his cabin. Blackwood was with him. Durham mentioned several ships of which he had knowledge, and praised the noble conduct of some of the frigates. But 'the captain of the *Euryalus* hinted that there had been a want of exertion on the part of some particular ship.

'Collingwood started up and said: "Sir, this has been a glorious victory for England and for Europe – don't let there be a reflection against a cabin boy." ' 'This,' added Durham, 'quite silenced the captain of the *Euryalus*.'

Durham then left the cabin, and going on deck saw a French officer leaning on the capstan. He entered into conversation with him, and found it was Villeneuve.

The admiral said to Durham: 'Sir, were you in Sir Robert Calder's action?' Durham said that he was, and that he had commanded the ship which had discovered the Combined Fleet. Villeneuve sighed and said: 'I wish Sir Robert and I had fought it out that day. He would not be in his present situation, nor I in mine.'

Robinson of the *Euryalus* was still more particular about Villeneuve, whom he described as 'a tallish thin man, a very tranquil, placid, English-looking Frenchman; he wore a long tailed uniform coat, high and flat collar, corduroy pantaloons of a greenish colour, with stripes two inches wide, half boots with sharp toes, and a watch chain with long gold links'. Magendie on the other hand was 'a short, fat, jocund sailor, who found a cure for all ills in the Frenchman's philosophy, "*Fortune de la guerre*".'

Villeneuve's retinue were accommodated some days after the battle in the comparative comfort of the *Neptune*. Captain Fremantle wrote to his wife on October 28th to say that he was that instant towing the *Victory*, and that Collingwood 'has just made the signal for me to go with her to Gibraltar', though he later changed his mind, and Fremantle was ordered elsewhere. 'Admiral Villeneuve was with me on board over two days,' he continued. 'I found him a very pleasant and Gentlemanlike man, the poor man was very low ... but I still have the pleasure of feeding and accommodating his Captain and his 2 Aid du Camps and his Adjutant General, who are true Frenchmen, but with whom I am much amused.... I have found also an excellent French cook and a true Spanish pug-dog. ... These Frenchmen make me laugh at the gasconade as well as at their accounts of Bonaparte, the Palais Royal, Paris etc.... The French Captain drinks your health regularly every day at dinner. The poor man is married and laments his lot; one of the younger ones is desperately in love with a lady at Cadiz and Frenchmanlike carries her picture in his pocket. ...'

Fremantle's pug, which quickly grew attached to him, and long served to help alleviate the boredom of future service on blockade, had been another animal snatched from the *Santissima Trinidad*.

Another Frenchman happily accommodated was Infernet of the *Intrépide*, who had fought so gallantly and became the guest of Codrington in the *Orion*. Codrington found him 'much like us in his open manner, a good sailor and . . . he has more delicacy in his conduct, although perhaps boisterous in his manner, than any Frenchman I have before met with'. Codrington asked his wife to supply Infernet's wants when he reached England on parole, while Captain Hallowell of the *Tigre*, a particular friend of Nelson's, 'although not in the action, insisted on sending him a trunk with two dozen shirts, stockings, a bed, and some cloth to make a coat, and a draft for £100, as an acknowledgement of the civility he met with from Ganteaume and his officers when a prisoner'. Infernet remarked to Codrington, of the censure on Sir Robert Calder: 'It is very well for you gentlemen that you can feel justified in finding fault with an admiral who, when in command of *fifteen* sail of the line fights a battle with *twenty*, because he only makes two of them prizes!'

7

Afterwards

IT IS A COMMONPLACE in the history of warfare
that victory is rarely exploited to the hilt. The victors are
too exhausted by battle, too weakened by losses, too satisfied with the fact that they have won. In Nelson's time it
had been as true of sea action as of land, though there had
been some notable exceptions.

Nelson himself had sometimes talked of a 'Lord Howe
victory', despite his reverence for that seaman: his feeling
that the Glorious First of June had been a strategic failure,
and only a half-developed tactical success, was shared by
many officers who studied their profession closely; while
his admired friend Lord Hood had made his anger all too
apparent when Rodney had failed to turn the battle of the
Saints into one of annihilation.

Through one of his early captains, William Locker, Nelson was a pupil of Hawke, and when Nelson was still in the
cradle, Hawke, by his majestic victory of 1759 at Quiberon
Bay, won on a stormy November day off an iron coast, had
shown how success could be consummated. The fleet commanded by Conflans, to which Hawke was opposed, ceased
to exist. Even in his old age, Hawke felt the same as ever
about naval warfare. 'For god's sake,' he wrote to a friend
in 1780, when Nelson was a junior captain, 'if you should
be so lucky as to get sight of the enemy, get as close to
them as possible. Do not let them shuffle with you by engaging at a distance, but get within musket shot if you can;
that will be the way to gain great honour, and will be the
means to make the action decisive.'

Hawke had not lived in vain, and there had in fact been
other instances of thorough fulfilment within Nelson's life-

time, notably Duncan's victory at Camperdown in 1797, which had crippled the Dutch fleet, then in the service of France. Above all, there was his own feat at the Nile.

Collingwood, tried as he was by the events of October 21st and the storm which followed, never for one moment lost his grip of the strategic as well as the tactical situation, never relaxed, never tolerated negligence in his captains, either in principle or in detail. So far as the wider campaign was concerned, there were still loose ends, which must be attended to. He thought at first that Dumanoir had entered Cadiz with Gravina and Cosmao, and kept inshore watch on that port until it was certain that the Frenchman was elsewhere, when the strength of blockaders was decreased. Again, Allemand was still at large, and it was even possible that he might appear from the west, though the chances of such a bold course were not great. Above all, there was Craig and his Italian expedition to be supported and kept informed, and Pitt's whole policy to be implemented.

One of Collingwood's earliest Trafalgar dispatches was to Elliot at Naples, and it is certain that, had Nelson lived, he would have written in much the same terms and with quite the same speed. 'As it is of great importance,' he wrote, 'to the affairs of Italy and Europe in general that the events which have lately taken place on this coast should be known as soon as possible at the Court at which you reside, I lose no time in informing you, Sir, that on the 19th instant the Combined Fleet sailed from Cadiz, their destination certainly for Italy.' Collingwood then described the battle, 'the most decisive and complete victory that ever was gained over a powerful enemy', and the escape of Dumanoir to the south. 'I will venture to say,' he added, 'had the battle been fought in the Ocean far from land and unembarrassed by the rocks and shoals of Gibraltar, there probably would not one of the enemy's ships have escaped.' He concluded: 'As soon as I can make the necessary arrangements, I propose coming into the Mediterranean, and if the Spanish squadron of Cartagena is in motion and at sea, to use my utmost endeavours to destroy them also and send to the Italian coast such a force as will check any operations the enemy may have in contemplation there.'

Elliot and the Court of Naples could now be assured that there could be no possibility of serious interference at sea in the immediate future. Collingwood's own detachments would continue to watch what he called the 'Spanish beauties' at Cartagena, for although no threat seemed likely to come from that place, the Fleet was well provided, and British seamen, with appraising eye, could never withhold admiration for Spanish ship-building, which had established a pattern of excellence such as was the envy of most shipyards.

Collingwood, in fact, took over all Nelson's burdens. While he lived, he was never to be relieved of them, and five weary years were to pass before he joined his friend in the crypt of St Paul's.

11

It was Sir Richard Strachan, henceforward to be known to contemporaries, from a sentence in his dispatch, as 'the delighted Sir Dicky', who added four more to the depleted prizes of Trafalgar. Earlier in the campaign he had rendered notable service in warning Orde of Villeneuve's escape from the Mediterranean. He was to add a sparkling pendant to the events of the battle.

Dumanoir, after leaving the stricken scene, had made for Gibraltar, but had not entered the Straits. On October 22nd the southerly gale had struck his damaged squadron, and he had found it impossible to stand up to it. Then, towards evening, he saw sails which he believed to be Rear-Admiral Louis and his ships, and he decided to reach to the westwards, in the hope of falling in with Allemand. For two days he searched for him, doing the best he could to repair his sails and stop his leaks, and then, on the 25th, he decided to go northward. On the 29th, as Louis was on the point of joining Collingwood, Dumanoir doubled Cape St Vincent. Neutrals were questioned, but not a word of Allemand could be had. Dumanoir therefore stood on for Rochefort, unaware that Strachan was ahead of him.

Strachan had remained in constant touch with the cruiser-line off Vigo until the day of Nelson's battle. Then, hearing that the ships which Villeneuve had left in Vigo were ready for sea, he moved away to let them out. On October 24th he took station off Finisterre, convinced that, with Nelson before Cadiz, the enemy must go north. He was thus well placed to intercept Dumanoir, of whose presence at large he was, of course, quite unaware.

As for Dumanoir, his ships were making so much water that he was forced to keep near the coast. He passed Finisterre early on November 2nd, inshore of Strachan, without being sighted – but his luck then failed him. Captain Thomas Baker of the *Phoenix*, a skilled and successful frigate officer who had already had a lion's share of fighting and excitement, was once again at the right place at the right moment. He had been rewarded for good service by the opportunity of a lucrative detached cruise, but had heard news of Allemand through a Danish skipper. The information was false, but it suggested that Allemand was somewhere in the Bay of Biscay, making for his home port of Rochefort. Baker flung the certainty of prize-money to the winds, and made straight for Ferrol, where he expected to meet Strachan. Not finding him there, he headed for the Finisterre rendezvous, and at daylight on November 2nd discovered himself inshore of what he believed to be Allemand's squadron, but what in fact was Dumanoir's.

The French admiral detached the *Duguay-Trouin* to chase the *Phoenix*, but Baker, instead of trying to escape, held on for Strachan's rendezvous. The *Duguay-Trouin* failed to cut him off, and he was soon in sight of Sir Richard.

Baker was fired on before he could make his identity clear to Strachan in the *Caesar*. When he had done so, he reported that he had just been chased by Allemand, and that the French were close by, to leeward. 'I was delighted,' wrote Strachan, in words which echoed round the Fleet, 'and told him to tell the captains astern that I meant to engage at once.'

The *Phoenix* sailed away to rally the squadron, while Strachan held on after the chase. He sighted the French in the moonlight, standing away in line abreast, but when the moon set, they were free to alter course, safe from observation. Dumanoir altered to south-east, towards Cape Ortegal. Strachan was not deceived. He waited for two of his 74's to join him, the *Hero* and the *Courageux*, together with one more frigate, Lord William Fitzroy's *Aeolus*, and headed in the same direction. He had reasoned that Dumanoir would probably try to slip into Ferrol, and he was right.

By daybreak on November 3rd, with another frigate, the *Santa Margarita* added to his force, Strachan had Dumanoir once more in sight. The British were soon to be joined by the *Phoenix* and the *Revolutionnaire*, a heavy frigate taken from the French, and as the *Phoenix* was bringing up the *Namur*, the last of Strachan's big ships, Strachan was in the happy position of having four ships of the line, to oppose an equal number of the enemy, besides which he had the help of four frigates. For once, the frigates could play an essential part in an action between big ships, and they could, indeed, tip the scale decisively.

All day the chase continued, and as Strachan's position prevented any possibility of Dumanoir making Ferrol, his direction was across the Bay towards Rochefort, with the British slowly gaining. The night was fine, and Strachan was able to keep Dumanoir in sight throughout. By the morning of November 4th the *Caesar*, Strachan's flagship, and the *Scipion*, Dumanoir's rear-most vessel, were barely six miles apart.

The British frigates were well ahead of the ships of the line, and were just within gunshot. As early as six o'clock the *Santa Margarita* and *Phoenix* had got near enough to give the *Scipion* their broadsides, though Dumanoir was still hoping to be able to avoid an action. He had had to jettison a number of guns to keep his flagship seaworthy, and was in no condition to fight an inferior force, much less the one which was now hard on his heels. But by eleven o'clock he had no choice. The *Scipion* was unable to drive off the frigates, and was beginning to suffer badly, so Dumanoir hauled to the wind in line of battle. Action became as inevitable as it had been when Villeneuve took the same course at Trafalgar, and expectations on both sides were much the same.

When Strachan saw the movement of the enemy, he had only three of his heavy ships up with him. He hailed his captains to tell them that he intended to attack the enemy centre and rear. He himself led into action with the *Caesar*, which was the most powerful vessel he had with him – once again, an echo of Trafalgar was apparent.

The usual practice in such a situation was for the leading ship to engage the enemy's windward vessel, and for the second astern to pass on, under cover of her fire, and to make for the next ahead, the process being repeated down the line. Strachan did not do this, probably because Dumanoir was second in the French line, and Strachan wished to bring the flagships together. Like Nelson, he wished to seek out the enemy commander.

In the action which followed, the frigates, instead of taking up the more orthodox position to windward of their own force, placed themselves to leeward of the *Scipion*, and continued to engage her. They hoped to take a full part in what could scarcely fail to be a successful encounter.

Strachan secured a concentration on the rear, but left the van ship, the *Duguay-Trouin*, disengaged. Dumanoir promptly signalled for his squadron to tack in succession, his intention being to cover his rear, which was in acute danger, and perhaps to cut off the *Namur*, which was now seen approaching. It was a bold move. It had to be done under a destructive fire from the *Caesar* and the *Hero*, and it brought the French within pistol shot of the British line.

Strachan had difficulty in turning, and for more than half an hour action ceased. Seeing that the French might weather him and get away, Strachan ordered the *Namur* to bear up and engage the French van – alone. Of his other three ships, the *Hero* got round first, and Strachan ordered her to lead. Action was renewed with a fresh attack on the French rear, the frigates keeping their position astern and to leeward. Presently the *Namur* was able to place herself in line, behind the *Hero*, and – the *Duguay-Trouin* being by this time out of action – Strachan's four battleships could concentrate on the other three. 'The French squadron fought to admiration,' said Strachan in his dispatch, 'and did not surrender until their ships were unmanageable.' But by four o'clock all was over, and by nightfall all the French ships were in Strachan's possession.

It was not until Dumanoir came on board the *Cæsar* that Strachan knew whom he had been fighting. 'Judge of my surprise,' he wrote, 'when I found the ships we had taken were not the Rochefort squadron, but four from Cadiz.' Allemand's movements were still a mystery, but Strachan had the satisfaction not only of taking four useful vessels, one of which, the unlucky *Duguay-Trouin*, survived until after the Second World War as HMS *Implacable*, a notable example of French shipbuilding, but he heard at least the general outcome of Trafalgar. Collingwood's official dispatch in fact reached England just about the time that Strachan's Biscay action was ending. Soon after the news of his success reached London, Strachan found himself promoted Rear-Admiral of the Blue, though this was in the ordinary course of seniority. For his services against Dumanoir he was given the star of the Bath, and a pension of £1,000 a year. He had every reason to be delighted, but although he showed himself a skilful tactician, the result could never have been in doubt.

Strachan had a way with words, not unlike Nelson's. He was also generous in praise of his people. 'I have returned thanks to the Captains of the Ships of the Line and the Frigates,' he wrote, 'and they speak in high terms of approbation of their respective Officers and Ships' Companies. If anything could add to the good opinion I have already formed of the Officers and Crew of the *Caesar*, it is their gallant conduct in this day's battle. The enemy suffered much, but our ships not more than is expected on these occasions.'

The British casualties were twenty-four killed and over a hundred wounded. Strachan commented: 'I dare say Their Lordships will be surprised we have lost so few men. I can only account for it from the enemy firing high, and we closing suddenly.' The French lost heavily in men, particularly in the *Scipion*, which suffered 111 killed and wounded, a sign of the efficient work of the frigates.

The makers of popular songs and ballads, full as they were of the death of Nelson, did not overlook Strachan, and to the fine old tune of 'Heart of Oak' (composed originally in honour of Hawke) they put some new words.

Though with tears we lament our great Nelson's demise,
Let the nations rejoice that more Nelsons arise;
'Twas Collingwood finished what the hero begun
And brave was the conquest accomplished by Strachan.

The rhyme at least has the merit of showing how the man in the street pronounced Strachan's difficult name.

With the disposal of Dumanoir, the immediate naval campaign was over, for the few remaining ships in Cadiz, though they continued to be watched, proved no further use in the war, and the surviving French vessels were handed over when Spain changed sides, three years later. Only Allemand remained at large.

Just before Trafalgar, this intrepid admiral had decided to run for the Canaries, in the hope of injuring British trade. Within a fortnight he was close to Teneriffe, and on the day that Strachan met Dumanoir he was being made welcome by the Spanish garrison. He stayed some days, landed his sick, re-victualled, sold his prizes, and then gave out that he intended to cruise in the neighbourhood of Madeira, after which he would proceed to the coast of Portugal, where he hoped to disorganize the British lines of communication.

After three days, he captured a British merchantman, outward bound, and learnt from her captain that before leaving Portsmouth he had heard a rumour that a great battle had been fought, and that Nelson had been killed. Allemand reasoned that if this were indeed so, the coast of Portugal might be less well guarded than it had been for some time, and his arrangements held.

In mid-December he took three small prizes. He learnt from them that there was a powerful squadron on the look-out for him, and that Nelson and Strachan between them had annihilated the Combined Fleet. 'The indiscretion of those who brought me the news struck consternation aboard, and aroused keen anxiety to get into port,' wrote Allemand. This was not surprising, and his own luck held till the last. Thick weather helped him to elude the net-work of watchers, and he ran into the safety of Rochefort on Christmas Eve, 1805. His foray, which had caused so much disturbance to the Admiralty in London, and so much loss among the British trade, proved how right Decrès had been when he had urged Napoleon not to plan

in terms of large-scale naval movements, but to engage in
war against commerce, conducted by small and efficient detachments. Allemand had shown the way.

III

It was the *Pickle* schooner, one of the smallest ships at
Trafalgar, commanded by a lieutenant of French descent,
which brought official news of the battle to London. The
Pickle was fast, she had done well in rescue work after the
action, and Lapenotiere, who was in charge of her, was a
favourite with Collingwood. Blackwood had hoped for the
chance to be sent, but the *Euryalus* was too useful to be
spared for the time, and her captain had to be content with
carrying home the principal French and Spanish prisoners,
a later honour sufficient in itself.

The *Pickle* had sight of land on November 4th, and
Lapenotiere was able to land at Falmouth early next day.
He posted at once to London, made extraordinarily good
time, considering the season of the year and the state of the
roads, and arrived at the Admiralty at one o'clock in the
morning on November 6th.

On her way north, the schooner had fallen in with the
frigate *Nautilus*, and had given her captain the news. The
Nautilus had put into Lisbon, and had been sent home by
the British Consul with urgent dispatches. Sykes, her captain, made an exceptional passage to Plymouth, and managed to reach Whitehall at the same moment as Lapenotiere, who was promoted to the rank of commander.

This time Marsden, the Secretary of the Admiralty,
made no mistake, though no immediate re-disposition of
forces was involved. Barham was in bed and asleep, but he
roused him personally, and gave him the news at once, as
architect of the great campaign. Secretary and First Lord
then summoned all the clerks who could be found, and
spent the rest of the night making copies for the King, for

Pitt, and for the *London Gazette*. Private messages were sent to Nelson's brother, to Lady Hamilton at Merton, and to Lady Nelson, who received a note in Barham's own hand.

Collingwood's dispatch was printed in *The Times* in its issue dated Thursday, November 7th, by which time the main outline of events had been circulated by word of mouth in the countryside through which Lapenotiere and Sykes had ridden, and in the metropolis itself. It was a time when London crowds were capable of much more violence and disorder than is ever seen today, but for once the nation was sobered in its triumph by a sense of irreparable loss. Lord Malmesbury declared that 'not one individual who felt joy at this victory, so well-timed and complete, but first had an instinctive feeling of sorrow. I never saw so little public joy. The illumination seemed dim, and as if it were half clouded by the desire of expressing the mixture of contending feelings; every common person in the streets speaking first of their sorrow for Nelson, and then of the victory.'

Barham, old as he was, had done his work, and could face retirement with equanimity. He was in fact soon out of office, returning to an obscurity which long concealed his immense services to the country, and which even today are recognized mainly by historians, since his role was unspectacular and administrative. Though this was so, he was none the less the brain behind every movement of the Fleets, and to the conduct of the naval war he brought the experience of a lifetime, and a devotion to his profession which was not exceeded even by Nelson and Collingwood, who were his instruments.

As for Pitt, at the very centre of affairs, he had known Nelson personally for many years, he had seen him at length during his last visit to London, and he felt his loss in the way that all men did who had ever fallen beneath his spell, Malmesbury happened to dine with him the day after he received the news. Pitt was then himself on the verge of his last illness, but active as always. 'I shall never forget,' said Malmesbury, 'the eloquent manner in which he described his conflicting feelings when roused in the night to read Collingwood's dispatches. Pitt observed that he had been called up at various hours in his eventful life by the arrival of news of various hues, but that, whether good or bad, he could always lay his head on his pillow and sink into sound sleep again. On this occasion, however, the great event announced brought with it so much to weep over, as well as to rejoice at, that he could not calm his thoughts, but at length got up, though it was three in the morning.'

The effect on George III, when he read the dispatch at Windsor, was perhaps even more remarkable. He was silent for the space of about five minutes, which must have caused consternation among his entourage. Then he summoned the Queen and the Princesses, had the news read to them, and ordered that a Thanksgiving Service should be held in St George's Chapel.

8

Apotheosis

EVERYTHING CONSPIRED to make Trafalgar different from and more conclusive than any earlier battle under sail. In one sense it was the naval counterpart of Waterloo; in another, it was even more the end of an era, since, while the British soldier continued to engage in set-piece encounters throughout much of the nineteenth century, the next full-scale fleet action in which the Royal Navy would be involved – that off Jutland, in 1916 – was fought under circumstances which bore only the faintest resemblance to earlier naval warfare.

If it should have need to fight them, the navy of an island power must always win its battles first, otherwise its soldiers cannot be transported in safety to the countries where they will meet the enemy. The principle is timeless; and Trafalgar helped to make Waterloo possible. It was won almost ten years earlier than the land battle, and the two events may seem to have no other connection, except as illustrating the art of the admiral and that of the general, exercised in full flower by the two men who represented, for Englishmen, all that was highest in leadership against Napoleon.

Because Trafalgar was won so early in the renewed war with France, it seemed at the time to have affected little. The country had grown used to having its way afloat. A sea victory was nothing new, however grand, tragic or triumphant its details. Soon after the news came that Nelson was dead, it became known that Pitt was dying, and it seemed that his Third Coalition against France, the combination of Great Britain, Russia, Austria and Sweden, might be no more effective than earlier combinations. The capitulation of Ulm was followed, in less than two months, by the Battle of Austerlitz, by the end of the ancient Holy Roman Empire, by the alliance of Prussia with Napoleon, and by the eclipse of Austria as a military power. Pitt lived to hear the dismal news, and died broken-hearted.

Trafalgar in fact seemed doubly disappointing, first by reason of Nelson's loss, and again because there appeared to be so little to show for it. Even at the time when the Press was full of the battle, it was also loud with a possible threat to Hanover, a matter which affected George III very closely, since he was Hereditary Elector.

The first and most obvious legend to establish was that Nelson had died to save his country from invasion. Although the facts were against it, they were not realized by the public at large, and such a cause did indeed appear great enough for the sacrifice even of such a paragon. It was allowed to pass for truth almost until our own day. It was comfort in loss, and such matters are not strictly susceptible to reason. It was at least true that Nelson had removed the last *possibility* of a threat to this country. There was now no fleet capable of making an attempt, even if Napoleon had been rash enough to revive his project.

There were various ways in which the edge of public disappointment could be blunted, and by which an aura of magic, such as still surrounds the battle, could be fostered. Trafalgar afforded, with its inevitability, its tension and its climax, the finest opportunity which had been given to artists since the death of Wolfe on the Heights of Abraham, in 1759, the 'Year of Victories', nearly half a century before, when the country was at a peak of greatness. It could be made the occasion of a splendid funeral, and it could show a new instance of how generously compatriots could endow the family of a national hero. Each of these possibilities was exploited to the full. Each helped to divert thoughts from a Continent where Napoleon seemed unassailable.

According to Benjamin West, the historical painter, Nelson himself had foreseen the possibility of legend. His retinue were familiar enough with his discourse on the liklihood of his losing another limb, and they all knew that, if he were killed, he would prefer to be buried in St Paul's rather than in the Abbey. He believed that the Abbey, having been built on a marsh, would one day disappear, while he thought that St Paul's, on its eminence, would last longer. West had a tale of his own to tell.

Shortly before his last campaign, Nelson and West had found themselves sitting next to one another at a public dinner. Nelson had none of the man of action's supposed indifference to artists, and he lamented to West that his own artistic education had been so limited. However, he added, there was one picture he admired beyond most others; it was West's *Death of Wolfe*. This was familiar to him through engravings. His friend Sir William Hamilton, an excellent judge, and in his younger days a close friend of Wolfe's, always commended it. Nelson asked West why he had done no more pictures of the same kind. 'Because,' said West, 'there are no more subjects.' 'Damn it!' exclaimed Nelson: 'I did not think of that!' A short pause followed, and Nelson then asked West to drink a glass of champagne with him, the wine he favoured. 'My Lord,' ventured the painter, 'I fear that your own intrepidity may yet furnish me with another such scene, and if it should, I shall certainly avail myself of it.' 'Will you?' said Nelson, pouring out bumpers. '*Will* you, Mr West? Then I hope I shall die in the next battle.'

The story may sound rather too good to be true, but West did in fact lose no chance when the time came, and Trafalgar gave him his 'new subject'. He even painted an Apotheosis, showing Nelson's heroic spirit being borne heavenwards by angels, Victory crowning him, and a beneficent Deity no doubt ready to welcome him to a peculiarly British version of heaven. This, if it were to please Nelson, would need to have resembled the famous naval dining club founded in 1765, of which he had been so appreciative a member.

Trafalgar had every concomitant upon which legend could be built. Those with a taste for history could point to the fact that it was fought in the very waters where, eight years earlier, Nelson had shown an extraordinary example of valour. At the time, he had been in charge of an inshore squadron blockading Cadiz. In thinking over the events of his life, he had this to say about an episode well known in the Navy. 'It was during this period,' he wrote in a sketch of his life which he provided for the Editors of the *Naval Chronicle*, 'that perhaps my personal courage was more conspicuous than at any other period. In an attack of the Spanish gunboats, I was boarded in my barge with its common crew of ten men, Cockswain, Captain Fremantle, and myself, by the Commander of the Gunboats. The Spanish barge rowed twenty-six oars, besides Officers, thirty in the whole; this was a service hand to hand with swords, in which my Cockswain, John Sykes (now no more), twice saved my life. Eighteen of the Spaniards being killed and several wounded, we succeeded in taking their Commander.' The whole incident had been prophetic, and Fremantle had even been with him again, closely in support, at Trafalgar. The battle had been fought not far distant from the scene of his exploits at Cape St Vincent, where he had won the star of chivalry – the Knighthood of the Bath – of which he was so proud. Moreover, Trafalgar was close to the gateway into the Mediterranean, where Nelson had made so brilliant a name in the opening phases of the war. It all fitted; moreover, the battle and its tragedy could be summed up in a sentence, as Frederick Marryat, novelist of Nelson's Navy, illustrated in a passage in *Poor Jack*, one of the best of his stories.

'We were abreast of Ram Head [says a pilot] when the men in another pilot-boat which had come out of

Plymouth and was close to us, waved their hats and kept away to speak to us. We hove-to for them.

' "Have you heard the news?" cried one.

' "No."

' "Lord Nelson has beat the French and Spanish fleet."

' "Glad to hear it – huzza!"

' "Lord Nelson's killed."

' "*Lord – Nelson's – killed!*"

'The intelligence was repeated from mouth to mouth, and then every voice was hushed, and the other boat hauled her wind without further communication. We did not at the time think of asking for any more. When the country awarded a public funeral to our naval hero, it did not pay him a more sincere tribute than was done in this instance by five pilots in a galley.'

11

Away off Spain in the *Victory*, one of Dr Beatty's first tasks, as soon as circumstances allowed, was to preserve Nelson's remains, for what everyone knew would be a state funeral. There was no lead out of which to make a coffin, so, said Beatty, 'a cask called a leaguer, which is of the largish size on ship-board, was chosen for the reception of the body; which, after the hair had been cut off, was stripped of the clothes except the shirt, and put into it, and the cask was then filled with brandy.'

'In the evening,' the account continued, 'after this melancholy task was accomplished, the gale came on with violence, and continued that night and the succeeding day without any abatement. During this boisterous weather, Lord Nelson's body remained under the charge of a sentinel on the middle deck. The cask was placed on its end, having a closed aperture at its top and another below; the object of which was, that as frequent renewal of the spirit

was thought necessary, the old could thus be drawn off below and a fresh quantity introduced above, without moving
the cask, or occasioning the least agitation of the body.'

Nelson was not the man to be placed in a cask of spirits
without at least a touch of drama. 'On the 24th,' said
Beatty, 'there was a disengagement of air from the body to
such a degree, that the sentinel became alarmed on seeing
the head of the cask raised.' For sheer under-statement,
this sentence must be hard to equal. The sentry was terri-
fied, and the rumour was soon flying round the decks that
the admiral was rising from the dead, angered, no doubt,
that his ships were not anchoring. 'The spirit was drawn off
at once,' said Beatty, 'and the cask filled again, before the
arrival of the *Victory* at Gibraltar on October 28th, where
spirit of wine was procured; and the cask, showing a deficit
produced by the body's absorbing a considerable quantity
of the brandy, was then filled up with it.'

After landing her badly wounded, and with the barest
essentials of repair to ensure reasonable safety for a long
voyage, the *Victory* re-passed the Straits mouth early on
November 4th, joined Collingwood's squadron off Cadiz
next day, and after a passage protracted by bad weather,
anchored at Spithead, where, less than four months earlier,
Rose and Canning had bade Nelson farewell. By that time
Blackwood had reached Portsmouth with the *Euryalus* and
his eminent prisoners. He and Hardy at once arranged for a
message to be sent to Lady Hamilton concerning Nelson's
last codicil.

Late in December the *Victory* proceeded to the Nore,
where on the 23rd the Commissioner's yacht received the
body, now enclosed in a splendidly decorated coffin. With
bells tolling, minute-guns firing, and colours at half-mast,
the yacht made her way to Greenwich, for the Lying in
State in Wren's Painted Hall. Thirty-thousand people are
believed to have filed past, Dr Scott keeping ceaseless, self-
appointed vigil.

On January 8th, 1806, in a violent south-west gale, the coffin was brought by river to the Admiralty in a long procession, attended by nine admirals, five hundred Greenwich pensioners, and the Lord Mayor and Corporation of London in State barges. At Whitehall Stairs the body was received by Norroy King of Arms, with nine heralds and pursuivants.

Next day the funeral, the most elaborate within memory, made its slow way to St Paul's. The Chief Mourner was Nelson's old friend and patron, Sir Peter Parker, and he was followed by thirty flag officers and a hundred captains. The Royalty present included another old friend, the Duke of Clarence, with whom Nelson had served in the West Indies.

As so often, the most moving tributes were those not rehearsed. Dr Scott wrote afterwards to Lady Hamilton: 'One trait I must tell you; the very beggars left their stands, neglected the passing crowd, and seemed to pay tribute to his memory by a look. Many did I see, tattered and on crutches, shaking their heads with plain signs of sorrow. This must be truly the unbought affection of the heart.'

As the coffin was being lowered into the crypt, a party of sailors from the *Victory* each seized a piece of the white ensign, the largest of the ship's three flags which had been flown in battle, and kept it as their memorial. 'That was *Nelson*,' said Mrs Codrington, wife of the captain of the *Orion*, the rest was so much the Herald's Office.' But even the Heralds themselves were moved on this singular occasion, for Sir Isaac Heard, Garter King of Arms, after reciting Nelson's many titles of honour, as if conscious that the roll of words included no adequate description of the dead, added – in breach of all precedent – '*the Hero who in the moment of Victory fell, covered with Immortal glory. . . .*'

III

The steps taken to establish the Nelson family in the dignity of the earldom which was granted after Trafalgar to the admiral's surviving brother William, is an interesting story in itself, not without its irony. At one time William had wanted to be a naval chaplain, and had actually gone on one cruise in a frigate commanded by Horatio. But the life had not suited him, and he contented himself with the enjoyment of a family living, until, as the fame of his brother grew, he began to have hopes of loftier preferment. This came to him in the shape of a prebend's stall at Canterbury, begged for him by a sea officer whom it was an honour to please. Then, as the admiral rose in dignity from Knight of the Bath, to Baron and to Viscount, so did William's hopes grow, since he saw every prospect of becoming his brother's heir.

'I suppose all the public reward of money will go to the parson,' wrote Collingwood on New Year's Day, 1806, 'who of all the dull stupid fellows you ever saw, perhaps he is the most so. Nothing in him like a gentleman. Nature never intended him for anything superior to a village curate and here has Fortune, in one of her frisks, raised him, without his body and mind having anything to do with it, to the highest dignity. Ten years since it did not seem to be on the cards.'

Collingwood was right. William Nelson was indeed much as he suggested, and the sum of £90,000 which was granted by Parliament to buy him an estate, afforded him immense satisfaction. More than that, there was a pension of £5,000 a year to go with the title 'for ever', an edict which Parliament, after the Second World War, decided should be just under a century and a half. William, who had not been a poor man before, could not even find grace enough to suggest that his Stall should be relinquished in favour of the devoted Dr Scott, though Nelson himself had hinted something of the sort to his brother, in the event of William coming into the title. Nelson's sisters, who needed money more than William, were granted £15,000 apiece, while his widow, who survived until 1831, had a state pension of £2,000 a year.

Nothing whatever was done for Emma Hamilton or for Horatia, and this fact has long troubled the conscience of those who ponder these things. The story of Nelson's personal life was not altogether a happy one, since he had parted from his wife some years before his death, and had made no secret of his devotion to the widow of his friend Sir William Hamilton. But in fact, Nelson and Sir William had between them left Emma well provided for, by most standards. She should have had not less than £1,200 a year, two houses and a great deal of valuable furnishings. It was, however, not enough for her way of life. The state did nothing for her, she soon got into debt, and by the year of Waterloo, ruined by her own lack of discipline (and, it should be added, her reckless generosity to others), she died in poverty in Calais, after which Horatia was adopted by Nelson's younger sister, Mrs Matcham. Horatia married a country clergyman, and the little help which in the end came to her was at a time when her growing family needed to be launched into the world.

Collingwood was made a baron, but, by comparison with the Nelson family, he came off badly. His state pension was £2,000 a year for one life only, though if his wife survived him she was to have £1,000 a year, and his daughters £500 a year apiece. Collingwood had no son, and his plea that his peerage might descend through the female line was not attended to. He spent the rest of his career in the Mediterranean as Commander-in-Chief, unrelieved, his health slowly declining until the had worn himself out. In these last years he was at least able to keep a close watch over the interests of the British military force in Sicily, which remained in being for the rest of the year.

IV

Nelson was buried, his family elevated, and the *Victory* restored to the active Fleet, but that was by no means the end of Trafalgar. Of the artists who had come aboard the flagship even before she arrived at Spithead, Arthur William Davis would recreate the scene in the cockpit with verisimilitude and pathos, and at a later stage Turner would amass a series of sketches upon which he would work, with varying degrees of grandeur, for many years to come. Prints of the battle itself, some based on sketches by sea officers who had been present, soon multiplied, and enjoyed a ready sale.

All through the nineteenth century the cult of Nelson grew. While Emma Hamilton lived, there was always the possibility of some gross indiscretion, for she was as careless over her correspondence as she was in most other matters, and seems to have kept every letter she ever received; but no revelation of the more disputable episodes in Nelson's life checked the tide of admiration and gratitude which found its culmination in the middle decades, when the Napoleonic War began to be seen in proportion. It was then that Trafalgar Square was planned, as one of the focal points of the capital.

There were many suggestions as to how the Square could best be laid out, when, in 1840, the appropriate Committee came to consider the matter of a fitting public memorial to the nation's greatest admiral. Some objected to a column being built which might obstruct the view of the National Gallery from Whitehall. One planner thought that the column should be placed at the side of the Square, so as to leave room for an even higher one in the centre, in case a greater than Nelson should appear. Some members of the Committee favoured two columns, each a hundred feet high, one for Nelson and the other for Wellington, but as the Iron Duke was then still alive, it was felt that this might create an awkward precedent, particularly as he had at one time been highly unpopular as a politician. Alternative sites which were considered were the centre of St James's Square; Oxford Circus; the top of Portland Place; and Greenwich. There were already monuments at Portsmouth and at many other places.

At last it was agreed that Charles Barry's Square should be adorned by a column designed by William Railton, on which should stand a sculptured figure by Edward Baily. Originally designed to be over two hundred feet high, the height was cut down by thirty feet to prevent damage from high winds. The statue itself was sixteen feet high, on a pedestal of just over twelve feet. The material of the column was Aberdeen granite, with bronze bas reliefs, while the statue was of Portland stone, saturated with boiling oil.

All was ready by 1849, except for Landseer's lions, which were added nearly twenty years later. It was just at the time when Sir Harris Nicolas had completed his great seven-volume edition of Nelson's *Dispatches and Letters*, so that the hero's memorial, in its main outlines, was fixed.

Two further principal events remained, to help to render Trafalgar one of the best illuminated victories in history. The first was the restoration of the *Victory* to her war condition, and her establishment in permanent dry-dock at Portsmouth, in the earlier decades of the present century. The second was the foundation of the National Maritime Museum, which was designed to house all the principal relics of Nelson and other notable sailors which had graced the old Greenwich Hospital, together with many additions.

The literary memorial to Nelson and to Trafalgar continues. Some of the best and wisest words about Nelson were written by Joseph Conrad, who as a young man had himself sailed in the very waters where Nelson fought the Combined Fleets, and who had come to know them as few have done before or since his time. 'Other men there were, ready and able to add to the treasure of victories the British navy has given to the nation,' wrote Conrad in *The Mirror of the Sea,* at the time of the centenary of the battle. 'It was the lot of Lord Nelson to exalt all this glory. *Exalt!* the word seems to be created for the man.

'In a few short years he revolutionized, not the strategy or tactics of sea warfare, but the very conception of victory itself. And this is genius. In that alone, through the fidelity of his fortune and the power of his inspiration, he stands unique among the leaders of fleets and sailors. He brought heroism into the line of duty. Verily he is a terrible ancestor.'

Conrad may also have the last words about the era in which Nelson lived. 'Never more shall British seamen going into action have to trust the success of their valour to a breath of wind. The God of gales and battles, favouring her arms to the last, let the sun of England's sailing fleet and of its greatest master set in unclouded glory. . . . By the exertions of their valour our adversaries have but added a greater lustre to our arms. No friend could have done more, for even in war, which severs for a time all the sentiments of human fellowship, this subtle bond of association remains between brave men – that the final testimony to the value of victory must be received at the hands of the vanquished.'

9

Epilogue

IT IS SELDOM, after more than a century and a half, that fresh light is reflected on a great victory. By far the greater part of the descriptive material will have been published, worked over, discussed again and again. Any new details will be valued, if only because unknown hitherto, and they are as much as can reasonably be looked for.

It so happens that, within the last few years, the Navy Records Society has issued, under the editorship of Professor Michael Lewis, two volumes of *A Narrative of My Professional Adventures*, by Vice-Admiral Sir William Henry Dillon. The period covered is that between 1790 and 1839, including the whole span of the long war with France, in which Dillon himself played his part. There was actually a time when he himself might have served under Nelson, though the chance was missed; but he knew Emma Hamilton well, and actually stayed with her at Merton.

When the campaign of Trafalgar was unfolding, Dillon was an unhappy though not an uncomfortable prisoner-of-war in France. He was at Verdun. In October 1805, he and his fellow-prisoners had belated news of Sir Robert Calder's action of the previous July. Before any details came out, Dillon had a bet with a friend, Lord Yarmouth. The terms were that Yarmouth should hand over five *louis d'or* to Dillon, and receive one back for every ship taken by the British. 'I was, unluckily in this case, the gainer by three,' said Dillon sadly. Calder's two Spanish prizes were a meagre harvest from a general engagement between two sizeable fleets.

Then, in December, news of Trafalgar cheered those in

the fortress city. This is how Dillon describes its effect on an isolated community.

'I happened to enter the . . . Club about 11 o'clock one day, when one of the Committee came in with the English newspapers containing the account of Nelson's victory over the Combined Fleets of France and Spain. Lord Yarmouth, Col. Abercromby and several others of my friends seized hold of me as if by one accord, and, lifting me on the table, desired me to read in a loud voice the official report of that splendid victory. The most perfect silence having been secured, I communicated the details of Collingwood's letter to the Admiralty. When I had finished it, three hearty spontaneous cheers were given by at least one hundred members present, and those who were not near the table closed up and requested me to read the account a second time, which I readily agreed to do.

'I was then requested by Lord Yarmouth to explain the manner in which the battle was fought, as they did not understand the nautical description of the disposal of the two Fleets. I did so by placing a parcel of books that were lying on the table in the position of the adverse Fleets. We separated then, but, going out to the street, we met a crowd of French gentlemen who were anxious to know the reason of all that cheering. I told them of our victory, and they were sadly cast down on the occasion. My French friends overloaded me with questions. They allowed that they could not contend with us on the ocean. "We do not doubt," they said, "that you have triumphed. But that you should have taken and destroyed so many ships without your losing any is a case we cannot admit. Our seamen can fight as well as yours, and surely you do not mean to maintain that our shot has not sunk *some* of your ships?" My only reply was that they might see Lord Collingwood's official report for themselves, by which it was perfectly clear that they had lost twenty sail of the line: but not one on our side, either lost or taken, a British admiral not daring to send home a false report.'

With appropriate variations, that scene must have been repeated everywhere that Englishmen foregathered. It was representative of a time before multifarious and speedy means of communication had lessened the impact of even the most extraordinary news. It was the same after Waterloo. When the Duke of Wellington commissioned Wilkie to paint the well-known picture of the victory dispatch being read in London by the Chelsea pensioners, the result was so popular that the Royal Academy consented to a special rail being placed in front of the canvas, to keep back the crush of visitors.

So far as Trafalgar was concerned, Dillon had the chance, later, of discussion with no less an officer than Mathieu Prigny, Villeneuve's Chief of Staff, who had returned to his own country. Dillon said:

'He had been wounded at the Battle, and had been sent to take the waters of Barège, which had been beneficial in curing him. . . . I do not recollect at any period of my life having enjoyed a more interesting conversation than I did in that officer's company. I found in Capt. Prigny an amiable and well-informed officer who did not, at the meeting which took place between us, conceal any of the facts or principal incidents which occurred between the hostile Fleets on that important occasion.

'After a conversation that lasted until 2 o'clock in the morning, wherein the gallant Frenchman made the most satisfactory replies to all my questions, I at length, fearing that I had made too many, said in conclusion: "I am truly sensible of your polite attention in conveying to me the interesting details which you have so frankly given."

"Not in the least," he replied. "We did not gain the victory, and the truth will out in due time. Therefore it would be absurd to conceal the events as they really happened." "Well," said I, "one more question before we part. What was the act on the part of the British Fleet that made the greatest impression on your mind during the battle?" "The act that astonished me the most," he said, "was when the action was over. It came on to blow a gale of wind, and the English immediately set to work to shorten sail and reef the topsails, with as much regularity and order as if their ships had not been fighting a dreadful battle. We were all amazement, wondering what the English seamen could be made of. All *our* seamen were either drunk or disabled, and we, the officers, could not get any work out of them. We never witnessed any such clever manoeuvres before, and I shall never forget them." '

Prigny, with experienced eye, had seen into the heart of things. Battle was battle, but it was the maintenance of pressure, after tactical success, which brought final reward to sea-power as exercised by Nelson and his Navy.

In fact, Trafalgar was both sunset and dawn. It was the sunset of large-scale battles under sail, and it was the dawn of a supremacy at sea which held for more than a century. Its effect on world history was long-term, widespread and, surely, beneficent, since British naval power was used, in the main, as a means of maintaining peace.

When that supremacy was at last challenged, in the First World War, it held – narrowly. But by that time British strategy had been diverted to land warfare, an unnatural and hideously costly role in lives, material and wealth. The casualty figures in France and Belgium alone almost stagger belief that any country could endure them, much less survive them without permanent ruin. Sea-power, essential as ever, was not used to its best effect; and in the

Second World War, while it still held as shield and supply
to this country, sea supremacy, except in European waters,
could not always be maintained. Such are the existing circumstances of world power that it will never be regained.

Trafalgar was one of the great moments in the history of
a country small in size and circumscribed in means, and
not an ignoble one in that of Europe. Its abiding lesson is
in dedication of service: and the courage and endurance of
succeeding generations, facing the test of war, have shown
that it has not been forgotten.

Appendix I

COLLINGWOOD'S TRAFALGAR DISPATCH, begun on the day after the battle but not immediately completed, appeared in a *London Gazette Extraordinary*, dated Wednesday, November 6th, 1805, in the form of two letters to the Secretary of the Admiralty:

Euryalus, Off Cape Trafalgar, Oct. 22, 1805.

SIR,

The ever-to-be-lamented death of Vice-Admiral Lord Viscount Nelson, who, in the late conflict with the enemy, fell in the hour of victory, leaves to me the duty of informing my Lords Commissioners of the Admiralty, that on the 19th instant, it was communicated to the Commander in Chief, from the ships watching the motions of the enemy in Cadiz, that the Combined Fleet had put to sea; as they sailed with light winds westerly, his Lordship concluded their destination was the Mediterranean, and immediately made all sail for the Streights' entrance, with the British Squadron, consisting of twenty-seven ships, three of them sixty-fours, where his Lordship was informed, by Captain Blackwood (whose vigilance in watching, and giving notice of the enemy's movements, has been highly meritorious), that they had not yet passed the Streights.

On Monday the 21st instant, at day-light, when Cape Trafalgar bore E. by S. about seven leagues, the enemy was discovered six or seven miles to the eastward; the wind about West, and very light; the Commander in Chief immediately made the signal for the fleet to bear up in two columns, as they are formed in order of sailing; a mode of attack his Lordship had previously directed, to avoid the inconvenience and delay in forming a line of battle in the usual manner. The enemy's line consisted of thirty-three ships (of which eighteen were French, and fifteen Spanish), commanded in Chief by Admiral Villeneuve; the Spaniards, under the direction of Gravina, wore, with their heads to the Northward, and formed their line of battle with great closeness and correctness; but as the mode of attack was unusual, so the structure of their line was new; it formed a crescent, convexing to leeward, so that, in leading down to their centre, I had both their van and rear abaft the beam; before the fire opened, every alternate ship was about a cable's length to windward of her second a-head and a-stern, forming a kind of double line, and appeared, when on their beam, to leave a very little interval between them; and this without crowding their ships. Admiral Villeneuve was in the Bucentaure, in the centre, and the Prince of Asturias bore Gravina's flag in the rear, but the French and Spanish ships were mixed without any apparent regard to order of national squadron.

As the mode of our attack had been previously determined on, and communicated to the Flag-Officers, and Captains, few signals were necessary, and none were made, except to direct close order as the lines bore down.

The Commander in Chief, in the Victory led the weather column, and the Royal Sovereign, which bore my flag, the lee.

The action began at twelve o'clock, by the leading ships of the columns breaking through the enemy's line, the Commander in Chief about the tenth ship from the van, the Second in Command about the twelfth from the rear, leaving the van of the enemy unoccupied; the succeeding ships breaking through in all parts, astern of their leaders, and engaging the enemy at the muzzles of their guns; the conflict was severe; the enemy's ships were fought with a gallantry highly honourable to their Officers; but the attack on them was irresistible, and it pleased the Almighty Disposer of all events to grant his Majesty's arms a complete and glorious victory. About three P.M. many of the enemy's ships having struck their colours, their line gave way; Admiral Gravina, with ten ships joining their frigates to leeward, stood towards Cadiz. The five headmost ships in their van tacked, and standing to the Southward, to windward of the British line, were engaged, and the sternmost of them taken; the others went off, leaving to his Majesty's squadron nineteen ships of the line (of which two are first rates, the Santissima Trinidada and the Santa Ana,) with three Flag Officers, viz. Admiral Villeneuve, the Commander in Chief; Don Ignatio

Maria D'Alava, Vice-Admiral; and the Spanish Rear-Admiral, Don Baltazar Hidalgo Cisneros.

After such a Victory, it may appear unnecessary to enter into encomiums on the particular parts taken by the several Commanders; the conclusion says more on the subject than I have language to express; the spirit which animated all was the same; when all exert themselves zealously in their country's service, all deserve that their high merits should stand recorded; and never was high merit more conspicuous than in the battle I have described.

The Achille (a French 74), after having surrendered, by some mismanagement of the Frenchmen took fire and blew up; two hundred of her men were saved by the Tenders.

A circumstance occurred during the action, which so strongly marks the invincible spirit of British seamen, when engaging the enemies of their country, that I cannot resist the pleasure I have in making it known to their Lordships; the Temeraire was boarded by accident, or design, by a French ship on one side, and a Spaniard on the other; the contest was vigorous, but, in the end, the Combined Ensigns were torn from the poop, and the British hoisted in their places.

Such a battle could not be fought without sustaining a great loss of men. I have not only to lament, in common with the British Navy, and the British Nation, in the Fall of the Commander in Chief, the loss of a Hero, whose name will be immortal, and his memory ever dear to his country; but my heart is rent with the most poignant grief for the death of a friend, to whom, by many years intimacy, and a perfect knowledge of the virtues of his mind, which inspired ideas superior to the common race of men, I was bound by the strongest ties of affection; a grief to which even the glorious occasion in which he fell, does not bring the consolation which, perhaps, it ought: his Lordship received a musket ball in his left breast, about the middle of the action, and sent an Officer to me immediately with his last farewell; and soon after expired.

I have also to lament the loss of those excellent Officers, Captains Duff, of the Mars, and Cooke, of the Bellerophon; I have yet heard of none others.

I fear the numbers that have fallen will be found very

great, when the returns come to me; but it having blown a gale of wind ever since the action, I have not yet had it in my power to collect any reports from the ships.

The Royal Sovereign having lost her masts, except the tottering foremast, I called the Euryalus to me while the action continued, which ship lying within hail, made my signals – a service Captain Blackwood performed with great attention; after the action, I shifted my flag to her, that I might more easily communicate any orders to, and collect the ships, and towed the Royal Sovereign out to Seaward. The whole fleet were now in a very perilous situation, many dismasted, all shattered, in thirteen fathom water, off the shoals of Trafalgar; and when I made the signal to prepare to anchor, few of the ships had an anchor to let go, their cables being shot; but the same good Providence which aided us through such a day preserved us in the night, by the wind shifting a few points, and drifting the ships off the land, except four of the captured dismasted ships, which are now at anchor off Trafalgar, and I hope will ride safe until those gales are over.

Having thus detailed the proceedings of the fleet on this occasion, I beg to congratulate their Lordships on a victory which, I hope, will add a ray to the glory of his Majesty's crown, and be attended with public benefit to our country. I am, &c.

C. COLLINGWOOD.

Euryalus, off Cadiz, Oct. 24, 1805.

SIR,

In my letter of the 22nd, I detailed to you, for the information of my Lords Commissioners of the Admiralty, the proceedings of his Majesty's squadron on the day of the action, and that preceding it, since which I have had a continued series of misfortunes; but they are of a kind that human prudence could not possibly provide against, or my skill prevent.

On the 22nd, in the morning, a strong southerly wind blew, with squally weather, which, however, did not prevent the activity of the Officers and Seamen of such ships as were manageable, from getting hold of the prizes (thirteen or four-teen), and towing them off to the Westward, where I ordered them to rendezvous round the Royal Sovereign, in tow by the Neptune: but on the 23rd the gale increased, and the sea ran so high that many of them broke the tow-rope, and drifted far to leeward before they were got hold of again; and some of them, taking advantage in the dark and boisterous night, got before the wind, and have, perhaps drifted upon the shore and sunk; on the afternoon of that day the rem-nant of the Combined Fleet, ten sail of ships, who had not been much engaged, stood up to leeward of my shattered and straggled charge, as if meaning to attack them, which obliged me to collect a force out of the least injured ships, and form to leeward for their defence; all this retarded the progress of the hulks, and the bad weather continuing, determined me to destroy all the leewardmost that could be cleared of the men, considering that keeping possession of the ships was a matter of little consequence, compared with the chance of their fall-ing into the hands of the enemy; but even this was an arduous task in the high sea which was running. I hope, however, it has been accomplished to a considerable extent; I entrusted it to skilful Officers, who would spare no pains to execute what was possible. The Captains of the Prince and Neptune cleared the Trinidada and sunk her. Captains Hope, Bayntun, and Malcolm, who joined the fleet this moment from Gibraltar, had the charge of destroying four others. The Redoutable sunk astern of the Swiftsure while in tow. The Santa Ana, I have no doubt, is sunk, as her side was almost entirely beat in; and such is the shattered con-dition of the whole of them, that unless the weather moder-ates I doubt whether I shall be able to carry a ship of them into port. I hope their Lordships will approve of what I (having only in consideration the destruction of the enemy's fleet) have thought a measure of absolute necessity.

I have taken Admiral Villeneuve into this ship; Vice-Admiral Don Alava is dead. Whenever the temper of the weather will permit, and I can spare a frigate (for there were only four in the action with the fleet, Euryalus, Sirius, Phoebe, and Naiad; the Melpomene joined the 22d, and the Eurydice and Scout the 23d), I shall collect the other flag officers, and send them to England, with their flags (if they do not all go to the bottom), to be laid at his Majesty's feet.

There were four thousand troops embarked, under the command of General Cotamine, who was taken with Admiral Villeneuve in the Bucentaure.

I am,
C. COLLINGWOOD.

Appendix II

THE TWO FLEETS

Van or Weather Column – Vice-Admiral Nelson:
12 of the Line

GUN-SHIP		Killed	Wounded
100 *Victory*	Vice-Admiral Viscount Nelson, K.B.	57	75
	Captain Thomas Masterman Hardy		
98 *Téméraire*	Captain Eliab Harvey	47	76
98 *Neptune*	Captain Thomas Francis Fremantle	10	34
74 *Conqueror*	Captain Israel Pellew	3	9
74 *Leviathan*	Captain Henry William Bayntun	4	22
74 *Ajax*	Lieutenant John Pilford (acting)	2	2
74 *Orion*	Captain Edward Codrington	1	21
64 *Agamemnon*	Captain Sir Edward Berry	2	7
74 *Minotaur*	Captain Charles John Moore Mansfield	3	20
74 *Spartiate*	Captain Sir Francis Laforey, Bart.	3	17
100 *Britannia*	Rear-Admiral the Earl of Northesk	10	40
	Captain Charles Bullen		
64 *Africa*	Captain Henry Digby	18	37

Rear or Lee Column – Vice-Admiral Collingwood:
15 of the Line

GUN-SHIP		Killed	Wounded
100 *Royal Sovereign*	Vice-Admiral Cuthbert Collingwood	47	94
	Captain Edward Rotheram		
74 *Mars*	Captain George Duff	29	69
74 *Belleisle*	Captain William Hargood	33	93
80 *Tonnant*	Captain Charles Tyler	26	50
74 *Bellerophon*	Captain John Cooke	27	123

GUN-SHIP		Killed	Wounded
74 *Colossus*	Captain James Nicoll Morris	43	110
74 *Achille*	Captain Richard King	13	59
64 *Polyphemus*	Captain Richard Redmill	2	4
74 *Revenge*	Captain Robert Moorsom	28	51
74 *Swiftsure*	Captain William George Rutherford	9	8
74 *Defence*	Captain George Hope	7	29
74 *Thunderer*	Lieutenant John Stockham (acting)	4	12
74 *Defiance*	Captain Philip Charles Durham	17	53
98 *Prince*	Captain Richard Grindall	0	0
98 *Dreadnought*	Captain John Conn	7	26

Besides the above twenty-seven ships of the line, there were also present:

Frigate: *Euryalus* Captain the Hon. Henry Blackwood
   ,,   *Naiad* Captain Thomas Dundas
   ,,   *Phoebe* Captain the Hon. Thomas Bladen Capel
   ,,   *Sirius* Captain William Prowse
Schooner: *Pickle* Lieutenant John Richards Lapenotiere

Cutter:
  Entreprenante Lieutenant R. B. Young

The *Combined Fleet* was composed as follows:

FRENCH: 18 of the Line, 5 Frigates, 2 Brigs

GUN-SHIP		Killed	Wounded
80 *Bucentaure*	Vice-Admiral P. Ch. J. B. S. Villeneuve	197	85
	Captain Jean Jacques Magendie		
80 *Formidable*	Rear-Admiral P. R. M. E. Dumanoir le Pelley	22	45
	Captain Jean Marie Letellier		
80 *Neptune*	Commodore Esprit Tranquille Maistral	15	39
80 *Indomptable*	Commodore Jean Joseph Hubert	Two-thirds drowned	
74 *Algéciras*	Rear-Admiral Charles Magon		
	Captain Gabriel Auguste Brouard	77	143

GUN-SHIP		Killed	Wounded
74 *Pluton*	Commodore Julien M. Cosmao	60	132
74 *Mont-Blanc*	Commodore G. J. Noel La Villegris	20	24
74 *Intrépide*	Commodore Louis Antoine Cyprian Infernet	Half crew	
74 *Swiftsure*	Captain C. E. L'Hospitalier Villemadrin	68	123
74 *Aigle*	Captain Pierre Paul Gourrège	Two-thirds crew	
74 *Scipion*	Captain Charles Berenger	17	22
74 *Duguay-Trouin*	Captain Claude Touffet	12	24
74 *Berwick*	Captain Jean Gilles Filhol Camas	All drowned	
74 *Argonaute*	Captain Jacques Epron	55	137
74 *Achille*	Captain Gabriel de Nieport	480 casualties	
74 *Redoutable*	Captain Jean Jacques Étienne Lucas	490	81
74 *Fougueux*	Captain Louis Baudoin	546 casualties	
74 *Heros*	Captain Jean B. J. Remi Poulain	12	26

Frigates: *Cornélie, Hermione, Hortense, Rhin, Thémis*
Brigs: *Argus, Furet*

SPANISH: 15 of the Line

GUN-SHIP		Killed	Wounded
130 *Santissima Trinidad*	Rear-Admiral don B. Hidalgo Cisneros	216	116
	Commodore don Francisco de Uriarte		
112 *Principe de Asturias*	Admiral don Federico Gravina	54	109
	Rear-Admiral don Antonio Escano		
112 *Santa Ana*	Vice-Admiral don Ign. Maria D'Alava	104	137
	Captain don Josef Guardoqui		
100 *Rayo*	Commodore don Enrique Macdonell	4	14

GUN-SHIP		Killed	Wounded
80 *Neptuno*	Commodore don Cayetano Valdès	38	35
80 *Argonauta*	Commodore don Antonio Pareja	103	202
74 *Bahama*	Captain don Dionisio Galiano	75	66
74 *Montanez*	Captain don Josef Salcedo	20	29
74 *San Augustin*	Captain don Felipe Xado Cagigal	184	201
74 *San Ildefonso*	Captain don Josef Bargas	36	124
74 *San Juan de Nepomuceno*	Captain don Cosme Churruca	103	131
74 *Monarca*	Captain don Teodoro Argumosa	101	154
74 *San Francisco de Asis*	Captain don Luis de Flores	5	12
74 *San Justo*	Captain don Miguel Gaston	–	7
64 *San Leandro*	Captain don Josef Quevedo	8	22

Index